Tennessee County History Series

EDITORIAL BOARD

Frank B. Williams, Jr., Editor for East Tennessee
Robert B. Jones, Editor for Middle Tennessee
Charles W. Crawford, Editor for West Tennessee
J. Ralph Randolph, Coordinator

EDITORIAL STAFF
Anne B. Hurley

TENNESSEE COUNTRY HISTORY SERIES

McMinn County

by C. Stephen Byrum

Frank B. Williams, Jr.
Editor

MEMPHIS STATE UNIVERSITY PRESS
Memphis, Tennessee

Copyright © 1984 by Memphis State University Press

All rights reserved. No part of the book may be reproduced or utilized in any form or by any means, electronic or mechanical (including photocopying and recording) or by any information storage and retrieval system without permission from the publisher.

Maps prepared by MSU Cartographic Services Laboratory

Manufactured in the United States of America

Design by Gary G. Gore

ISBN 0-87870-176-1

TO PHYLLIS

Acknowledgements

This work has truly been a labor of love. It has given me the opportunity to explore my roots in a special way, and has provided the chance to add substance to that feeling of uniqueness that McMinn County has always provided for my life.

My hope is that this book has been written in such a way that not only trained historians and accomplished history "buffs" can profit from contact with it, but that school children and non-academics can be brought to have interest in and appreciation of their own geographical and historical backgrounds. Someone wisely remarked that it is difficult to know where we are going unless we have some idea of where we have been.

The thorniest problem in writing this book has been the decisions about what would be left out. It is certain that much more has been omitted than has been included. I hope that at some future time this material will become the basis for an exhaustive history of McMinn County. But space limitations and economic considerations notwithstanding, this material does represent the first specific attempt at an even relatively complete county history of this area.

I would like to acknowledge the assistance of all those who shared their personal reminiscences, and those whose often uncredited work appeared across the years in newspaper articles and retrospectives about the county that I have researched. Both *The Daily Post-Athenian* and the *Etowah Enterprise* have turned out excellent special edition histories in the last several years. I am particularly indebted to the writing of James Burn, Neal Ensminger, Frank McKinney, W. E. Nash, Grace Oliphant, and Mrs. Harold Powers in these papers. I am also indebted to the *DPA* for several of the older pictures that have been included. Burn, the McMinn County historian, made numerous helpful suggestions following his close reading of the original manuscript.

Those who have worked with this project at Memphis State University Press have been of utmost help. I am indebted to the advice and direction of J. Ralph Randolph. In addition, the exceptional editorial assistance of Frank Williams and Nancy Hurley has enhanced this material tremendously. My special gratitude must be expressed to them.

Most importantly, I appreciate the support of my family in this project. My son, Philip, did a good deal of the initial research on the Indian activities in the area. My daughter, Meredith, repeatedly provided "good company" on jaunts into the backwoods of the county to run down some lead or visit some site. My wife, Phyllis, has a gift for clarity of expression and what will be of lasting interest that has contributed immeasurably to the finished product. With great affection, I dedicate the work to her.

History is dynamic and most of it is lived out between the lines of that which finally is recorded in documents. This book is an affectionate look backward, a pause that allows us to remember—and in remembering, to see a "best" about ourselves that compels us to move into the future with renewed vitality.

A Preface of Wanderings and Personal Glimpses

When I think about McMinn County, I recognize that it has already taken on mythological proportions in my own mind—perhaps everyone's "home" does. It is sometimes difficult to sort out a myth, particularly in the South, and to preserve a sensitive tension between, on the one hand, the idea that this place that you care a great deal about is unique, and on the other, that there must be thousands of other small counties just like it—with similar histories and similar faces—from one end of this nation to the other. What our age desires is fact and not myth, but what we may need is feeling, too—so that the bones of the past can be given flesh and the cold vestiges of historical data, the faded, one-dimensional photographs of unremembered faces and unaccustomed styles can be warmed with memory and appreciation.

There is a distinct difference between history and heritage. Heritage is history that has somehow become personal. It is heritage that I am attempting to convey in these pages. More than to give a history of the county, I would like to convey something of the feeling of the place. If, beyond the data and the pictures, the names and the dates, there is created "a sense of place," then I will have been successful.

As I try to work back through the layers of my own myth, I see the photographs of Margaret Bourke-White in *You Have Seen Their Faces* and Walker Evans in *Let Us Now Praise Famous Men*. I, too, have seen the old Coca-Cola and Nehi signs with the thermometers built into the bottles, the walls covered with Cardui and Black Draught calendars, the faces which are shy before cameras but also proud of new, harnesslike overalls and blue serge suits. While I am sure that the pitiful poverty and degradation of the tenant sharecroppers captured by the photographs in the 1930s could have been found in McMinn County, on the whole it seemed always to be a more affluent, cleaner, less-given-to-extremes, and generally happier place than the highly dramatized, southern myths might suggest.

The Civil War did not rage here, although there were a few battles and skirmishes. There were few, if any, antebellum mansions of the Tara variety, although there were and are many fine homes. Neither the KKK nor the Civil Rights movement became items of major significance, although there have been moments of memorable division and conflict. From the county's inception there has been change, but like its waterways—the Hiwassee, Eastanallee, and Conestaga—it has almost always been calm, easy, consistent, and at times even touched with a marked beauty.

Another part of my personal myth grows out of the work of one of the greatest Tennessee literary figures, James Agee. Surrounding the plot of his epic *A Death in the Family* are human glimpses of Knoxville and East Tennessee in the early part of the 1900s. His description of the homes—"middle-sized gracefully fretted wood houses, with small front and side and more spacious back yards, and trees in the yards, and porches"—perfectly describes the finest dwellings which spread out from Washington Street and Madison Avenue, along Jackson Street across the bridge, and surrounding the college in the Athens of my youth. These were proud structures, like the people who lived in them, reflecting a precise attention to detail and craftsmanship which sometimes seems almost totally lost, unnecessary, or unaffordable in the sameness of the modern dwelling.

Agee's most poignant scene is of the summer evening ritual of men coming home from work, completing their evening meals, removing their starched white collars, and spending a good part of the early evening with hose in hand watering their lawns. With an almost religious precision the hose is uncoiled, the nozzle finely adjusted, the lawn given its nightly drink, and then the hose carefully recoiled and stored away.

> It is not of the games children play in the evening that I want to speak now, it is of a contemporaneous atmosphere that has little to do with them: that of the fathers of families, each in his space of lawn, his shirt fishlike pale in the unnatural light and his face nearly anonymous, hosing their lawns. These sweet pale streamings in the light lift out their pallors and their voices all together, mothers hushing their children, the hushing unnaturally prolonged, the men gentle and silent and each withdrawn into the quietude of what he singly is doing, peaceful, tasting the mean goodness of their living like the last of their suppers in their mouths; while the locusts carry on this noise of hoses on their much higher and sharper key.

Lawn is a curious word, a sophistication of *yard*, and certainly a far cry from the solid red-clay living spaces that surrounded settlers' cabins which were meticulously swept daily by the women as they also swept the dirt "floors" of the insides of their cabins. A lawn may have represented the first thing grown for decoration and not food; the spigot in the wall, quick and easy water that did not have to be laboriously carried in small amounts from a well, cistern, or spring. The evening ritual allowed the men, surrounded by *their* places and *their* families, a moment of meditative solitude.

In my earliest memories, my father stood there with his neighbors on summer evenings and watered his lawn. He and his neighbors were not dressed in the suspenders and collarless white shirts of Agee's Knoxville, but the matching green or gray of a factory foreman's uniform from Sears & Roebuck. He always paid careful attention to a pecan tree to mark the fact that he had lived in this place. My brother and I were put to bed with a Bible storybook that had served two generations, and the hissing of the hose became our lullaby. The sameness of the ritual gave security.

But, we always stirred when our mother left the room—to stare out across the semidarkness of neighbors' backyards to the Keith mansion which dominated the horizon and Highway 11 before there was a bypass and long before there was an interstate. We counted cars and dreamed of where they were going. We wondered what people did in mansions. We listened to the spray of hoses, and like many before and since found our own way of sinking indelibly imprinted roots of McMinn County deep into the subsoil of our existence.

Finally, my myth crosses the path of that superb Yankee poet, Wallace Stevens, and particularly his poem "Anecdote of the Jar." I have pondered it again and again from my own perspective as it has been informed by McMinn County.

> I placed a jar in Tennessee,
> And round it was, upon a hill.
> It made the slovenly wilderness
> Surround that hill.

> The wilderness rose up to it.
> And sprawled around, no longer wild.
> The jar was round upon the ground.
> And tall and of a port in air.
>
> It took dominion everywhere.
> The jar was gray and bare.
> It did not give of bird or bush,
> Like nothing else in Tennessee.

The poet wintered in Florida during the early middle of this century and traveled by train and car through Tennessee on his way South—perhaps I counted his car one night as I stared out my window. Tennessee, compared to the urban organization of his Connecticut home, was wildernesslike and came to represent a general chaos of life that needed focal points—like the jar—that could give definition and meaning.

I have always been troubled by Steven's analogy, especially in regard to McMinn County. Undoubtedly it was a wilderness when the first explorers under Hernando DeSoto came through the area in 1540. In many respects, the wilderness probably continued its existence through 1819 when the county was officially established.

But, a wilderness is not necessarily careless, untidy, or slovenly—to use Stevens' word. A wilderness is also a challenge and an opportunity, an unmolded piece of clay, for those who have the courage to take it into their hands and make something out of it. These kinds of people do not simply need focal points to provide meaning in the midst of chaos, the tenacity of their own lives *provides* and *becomes* a focal point. Their lives *impart* meaning, and squeeze creation out of chaos. These kinds of people founded counties like McMinn, becoming respectful inheritors of the past and responsible transmitters of the best of that past to the future.

In the fall of 1946 the most famous moment in the history of McMinn County took place. "The Battle of Athens" pitted newly-returned veterans, who had come to learn a new meaning of freedom in the hedgerows of France and the jungles of the South

Pacific, against the powerful political establishment backed by Shelby County's "Boss" Crump, one of the most powerful southern politicians since reconstruction. News of the "Battle," which will be described in detail in a later chapter, spread across the country, and inspired a series of such moments of "participatory democracy" in many locations.

Theodore White, famous for his volumes on the making of presidents, was dispatched by *Harper's Magazine* to chronicle the events. White's first impressions of the people and the county are revealing:

> The people of McMinn County, like the taut, coppery wires of the high tension lines which cross above them, hum with subdued peaceful activity until they are disturbed, and then, like the wires, they snap in a shower of sparks. The people are god-fearing. When the Robert E. Lee highway climbs out of the Shenandoah Valley, which can take its religion or leave it, into East Tennessee on the road to McMinn county the highway is sprinkled with signboards telling the godless wayfarers that "Jesus is coming soon" or warning them "Prepare to Meet God." McMinn itself is relatively free of such shrieking witnesses to faith. McMinn's religion is Methodist and Baptist, quiet, bone-deep, and sober. On Saturday afternoon when farmers throng the town, preachers are allowed to call sinners to repentance in the shade of the courthouse at the county seat. But most of McMinn meets God in the serenity of Sunday morning at the red brick or white board house of worship in peace and devotion. The church-goers have made liquor illegal, and Sunday movies are unlawful, too.

White's words were written almost forty years ago, and much of the physical landscape of McMinn County has changed. However, the "internal landscape" has varied little. Religion and politics continue their influences. Slogans may have changed and even made their way to bumper stickers on cars, but still the occasional cross formed in concrete announces that "Jesus is Coming." The power lines still hum with TVA power, although now from nearby nuclear reactors. There are Sunday movies, but liquor is still illegal and lawmen and bootleggers only occasionally continue their ironic roles.

"Moonshine" holds little more than a cultural and aesthetic significance, as the accessibility of Knoxville and Chattanooga has made the art useless and unprofitable. Every few years a liquor referendum is held and the church leaders rally the "forces of good" to face the "principalities and powers of the rulers of the darkness of the world." They continue to win by safe margins, and yet another periphery of the Kingdom of God is secured.

Another Tennessean, Alex Haley, wrote recently about "roots." Somewhere between the myth that has grown in my mind, the view from a windy ridge, and the quiet of an old mill stream, I find McMinn County. My roots, like those of many like me, are found there. This is our story.

MCMINN County covers 420 square miles of southeast Tennessee. It is characterized by wooded knobs, low ridges, panoramic vistas punctuated by the distant peaks of the Unakas and Great Smokies, and a life-giving system of seven major creeks which flow into the Hiwassee River along the county's southern boundary. The woodlands are full of game, the hills rich with ore, and the creeks a source of rich fertilization for the soil, energy for the operation of machines, and transportation.

It has been a place across the years where Indians, white settlers, and a few slaves did not simply survive but built lives that held every promise of being better in the future. For many, that promise has been kept; for many others, it continues to be renewed.

The English poet William Wordsworth was convinced that the essence of a place was not really captured until the beauty of the natural geography was experienced first hand. For Wordsworth this experience came from walking the countryside, and the rural backcountry areas in McMinn County can be traversed today with much the same impressions that the Indians and first settlers would have had two centuries ago. The county can be written about, and such writing will further knowledge about it; but to really be known, it must be walked, traversed

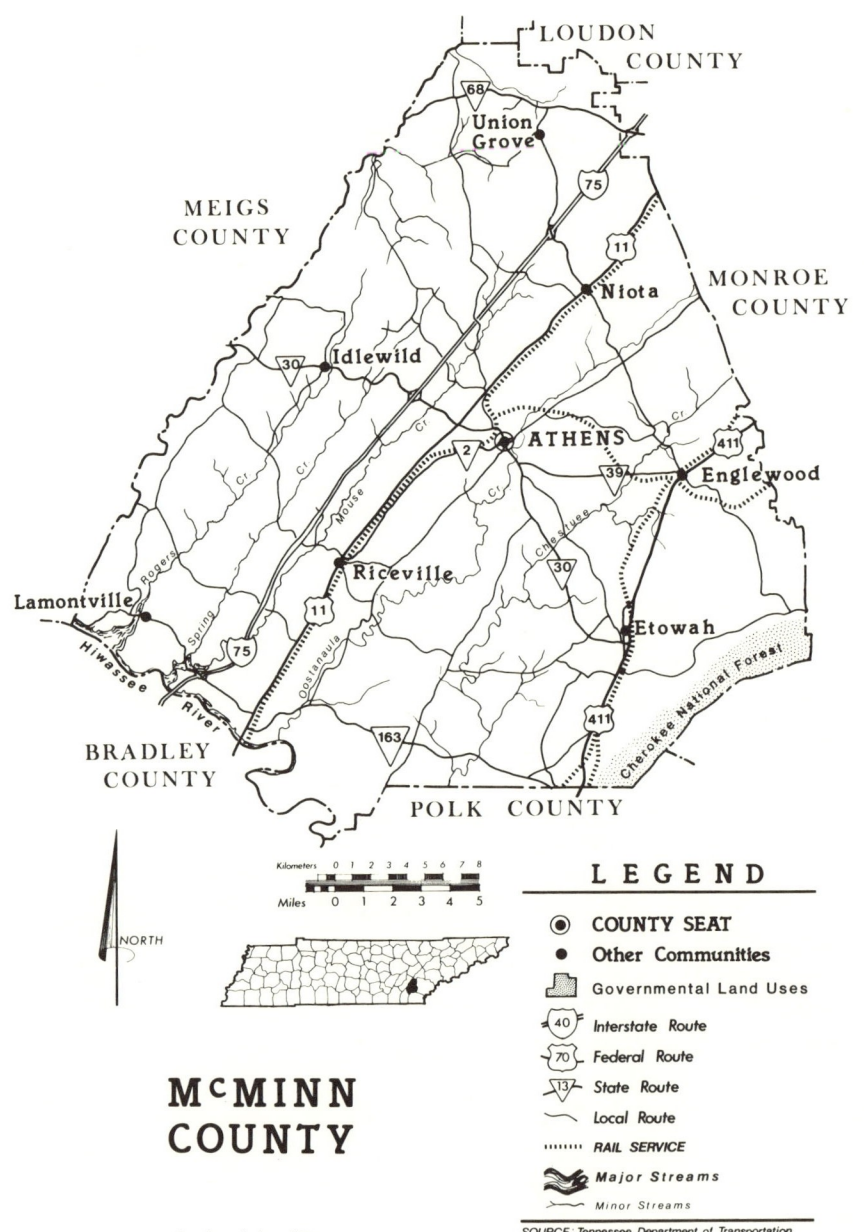

again and again, until it is experienced and known up close and personally.

The land is given its character by the Hiwassee River which forms its southern boundary, and by the mighty Tennessee River which flows within only a few miles of most of the county's western border. Six major creeks also wander across the landscape. Consequently, there are a series of ridges and sprawling creek valleys. The land is rich and often lush, making conditions ideal for the large farms that have existed since the earliest settlements. The streams made a variety of mill industries possible, and the rivers first provided efficient transportation and eventually the boon of cheap electrical power that attracted major industry in later years.

The best views are from the ridge tops, especially when the vistas spread out toward the east with Starr's Mountain and the Great Smokies rising as backdrops. The roads that lead out of Etowah and Englewood toward Tellico Plains and the northern part of Polk County pass through some of the most beautiful countryside in all of Tennessee—Mecca Pike is aptly named.

There are other byways that are well worth the time spent exploring: northeast of Athens through the Mayfield farms and the Mount Harmony community toward Madisonville; northwest of Athens along the Old Niota Road; from near the Meigs County line back through the valley to Riceville; the Piney Grove Road down toward Polk County and then back along what is now called the Bowaters Road to Calhoun. The streams must be fished, if only for the quiet that is still there and the occasional evidence of an old mill. Wordsworth would have loved it.

From Pre-Indians Days to the Cherokee Removal

There is no way to tell with precision how far back into history civilized life has existed along the banks of the Tennessee and major tributaries like the Hiwassee. The farmers who tilled the soil in the bottom land near Calhoun continually found skeletal remains and artifacts until the 1930s when the TVA dams were built.

In all likelihood there was habitation here as far back as perhaps 6000 BC; the period from 6000–1000 BC is often known as the Archaic Period. In other parts of the world at this time other river civilizations were also coming into existence, notably along the Nile in Egypt, the Tigris and Euphrates in the ancient Near East, and the Indus River valley in India.

A second period of likely habitation is known as the Woodland Period, and sometimes is referred to as the Wigwam Period because of the type of dwellings that were constructed. The people of this period, approximately 1000 BC–1000 AD, were primarily hunters. They are sometimes called "Mound Builders" because of their burial practices, and although no major mounds have been excavated in McMinn County itself, such mounds could easily be obscured, given the rolling nature of the countryside, erosion, and the growth of vegetation over a millennium or more.

Several years ago on an island near the mouth of the Hiwassee west of Calhoun two pieces of statuary closely resembling idols worshipped by the Aztecs of Mexico were discovered. The statues were characterized by wide open mouths just like the Aztec sacred icons. Since no North American Indians were supposed to be idol worshipers, it was generally assumed that these were artifacts left by DeSoto and his men as they moved through the area in the mid-1500s. However, it could as easily be that the artifacts were relics of some much-older civilization that touched the region.

Hiwassee Island, described in the sesquicentennial edition of *The Daily Post-Athenian* as "an island that parts the current of the Tennessee River where the yellow Hiwassee boils into it from the Big Smokes," is an intriguing place. Mounds as well as pyramidal buildings that housed an intricate worship system and were probably part of a culturally advanced community have been excavated here. In later years Sam Houston had a home there.

A more settled group of hunters and farmers, the Mississippi Indians, appeared around 1000 AD throughout the state. This group later evolved into the more specific Creek tribe in the east and Chickasaw in the west. The state was traversed by trade routes and warpaths, some that regularly carried tribal movements from as far away as Illinois and Florida. By 1700 the powerful Cherokee tribe, which is of greatest significance to McMinn County, migrated into the area from near the Great Lakes and drove the Creeks into Georgia. A lesser tribe, the Yuchi, from which the familiar Meigs County name Euchee is derived, was also forced to leave the immediate area.

The Cherokees had a tremendously complex society. They were careful managers of their environment, humane in the development of their tribal relationships, and sensitive to the need to educate their children. Some of the most important advances of native American civilization, such as the written language developed by the great leader Sequoyah in the early 1800s and a form of self-government modeled on that of the United States Constitution itself, were Cherokee. Although the Cherokees may have cooperated with the English in the Revolutionary War period, by the time of the wars against the troublesome Creeks and Chickamaugas, and the War of 1812 they were actively involved in the American advance.

One of the most significant battles of this period involved a McMinn County native Cherokee, John Walker, who will be discussed in detail later. The Creeks of Georgia and Alabama had rallied to the war cries of the British-inspired firebrand Tecumseh. On August 17, 1813, between 250 and 400 settlers were killed in the Fort Mims Massacre on the lower Alabama River in Georgia. As word spread of this event, 2500 men from the region, both white and Cherokee, volunteered—here the state of Tennessee got its nickname—to fight for Andrew Jackson. The great Cherokee chief, Junaluska, gave the support of his people to Jackson, and on March 27, 1814, at the Battle of Horseshoe Bend nearly one thousand Creek warriors were killed and the British-Indian alliance broken. John Walker, perhaps the most famous early McMinn Countian, was a major in Jackson's forces.

John Hart, a white settler from Roane County, was also a commander of part of Jackson's Tennessee volunteers, and was killed at Horseshoe Bend. His son, also named John, came to McMinn County as a youth and founded one of the county's oldest families. The white settler and the Cherokee native found many occasions to fight side by side.

As will be seen, it was mainly Cherokees who intermingled with the original white settlers in the area. There were numerous mixed marriages, and by the time written county records began to be kept it would have been difficult to find older McMinn County families that did not have some specific Cherokee lineage. This is especially true of those who settled in the Calhoun area. The Cherokee background is a proud aspect of the county's heritage, and from its inception one county high school athletic team has been appropriately known as "The Cherokees."

Hernando DeSoto was born soon after Columbus discovered the new world, and he spent his entire life consumed with ideas of discovery, exploration, and conquest. He was with Francisco Pizarro in Peru, and Inca gold and jewelry made him wealthy. In 1539 he used his fortune to finance an expedition to North America to find rumored cities of Indian gold and silver.

DeSoto was appointed governor of Cuba and Florida, which was the name used for the entirety of the southeastern United States. Many of the nearly 1000 men who accompanied DeSoto to America were ill-prepared to be frontiersmen; they were often affluent young Spaniards whose thirst for gold outweighed their good sense. DeSoto was so insecure about their ability to persevere in the new world that when they disembarked near present-day Tampa Bay he ordered the ships to return to Cuba.

It is difficult to know what word to use to describe DeSoto's journey through the Southeast. In a sense the men were explorers and discoverers, but in perhaps a more accurate view they were lost wanderers at the mercy of the environment and the Indians who often both befriended and harassed them. The best evidence suggests that crafty Indian chieftains discovered that promises of cities of gold farther along kept the Spaniards moving and kept them from being much more than a temporary inconvenience. An occasional Indian village was looted or burned, and there were occasional Indian raids; for the most part, the Spaniards wandered.

There is enough convincing evidence, however, in the chronicles of the journey to consider it a fact that DeSoto's men came into McMinn County. Sometime in 1540, the legend has it, the Spaniards camped on high ground overlooking Eastanallee Creek a short distance south of Athens. An old paper mill stood there in later years, and the site—its historical value well-established in the early settlers' minds—was considered a possible location for the first county seat. DeSoto died in 1541, and only about 300 of his men survived to float down the Mississippi River and find their way safely to Mexico.

Another early Spanish explorer, Juan de Pardo, came close to the area in 1566, building a small fort near present-day Chattanooga. By 1700 French traders regularly used the Tennessee and Hiwassee to move into the Carolinas.

Early Settlers

Significant European settlement did not occur until after the French and Indian War in the early 1760s when the territory west of the Appalachians to the Mississippi came under English control, and more particularly, as regards McMinn County, not until after the Revolutionary War and the Cherokee treaties of the early 1800s. The closest English outpost before this period was built in 1757 at Fort Loudon in present-day Monroe County, about 30 miles northeast of Athens, to protect Cherokee families from attacks by the French and their Indian allies. The primary link between people in this region and the outside world was through traders.

Historical records for the entire region from around the Revolutionary War until 1819, when the Cherokees ceded the Hiwassee District to the United States, are vague and incomplete. Between the Revolution and 1819 there was an influx of settlers. By the time the county seat was transferred from Calhoun to Athens in 1823 excellent court records and genealogical data began to be kept.

Perhaps a few representative examples of settlement, sketchy as they may be, can help to capture the spirit of this period. In this regard the Walker family history is of greatest significance, not only for McMinn County specifically, but because of its link to some of the most important personalities in the entire region.

With the exception of Sequoyah himself, Nancy Ward is perhaps the most famous Cherokee. She rivals Pocahontas and Sackajawea in importance. Her own tribe bestowed upon her the title "Beloved," the highest title that a woman could ever be given, which implied status equal to that of the chiefs themselves. The title conveyed almost mystical, divine powers—something equivalent to sainthood in modern vocabularies.

Nancy Ward first married an important chief named Kingfisher, and then an English trader named Bryan Ward. By Kingfisher she had a daughter, Catherine, who later married a white trader named John Walker. The free use of Christian names and the marriages that occurred with increased frequency demonstrates vividly the close relationship between English and Cherokee which was taking place in the mid-1700s.

John and Catherine Walker established a residence somewhere along the Hiwassee in the southwestern area of the county. They had a son who was also named John, and it is he who becomes the key figure. This John Walker captured the attention of Governor William Blount at the Battle of Buchanan Station in 1792. Blount wrote about Walker: "He has been raised among and by white people. Everyone who knows him has the utmost confidence in him. He is quite a stripling and apparently the most innocent, good-natured youth I ever saw."

The younger Walker, who had a strong enough Cherokee ancestry to be considered "Indian," married Elizabeth Sevier, the widow of Joseph Sevier, who was the son of John Sevier, governor of the shortlived state of Franklin and the first governor of Tennessee. Elizabeth herself was a member of an important Cherokee family. Walker helped organize the Cherokee Turnpike Company in 1806 that contracted to maintain the "Georgia Road" which ran through the area. He also operated a ferry near present-day Calhoun. At the outbreak of the War of 1812 he was commissioned a major and received numerous commendations for bravery in battle.

Following the war, Walker returned to Calhoun and was instrumental in all of the treaty negotiations which led to the surrender of Cherokee lands in Tennessee. These negotiations often took Walker and other major "chiefs" to Washington, or "Washington City" as it was called, where he met with luminaries of the federal government of that time, especially Secretary of War John C. Calhoun.

Several prominent Indians, who were deemed "capable" of managing their own affairs, and perhaps to reward their cooperation in the Hiwassee Purchase of 1819, were given choices of 640-acre plots which would be "reserved" for them in the newly acquired territory. Walker took his "reservation" at Walker's Ferry and this immediately was established as the town of Calhoun. Elizabeth Lowery Sevier Walker, after an unsuccessful attempt at acquiring land in present-day Monroe County, took land north of Calhoun at Pumpkintown.

In spite of a somewhat questionable reputation at the time, Pumpkintown was designated the county seat in December of 1823 and named Athens. The first organizational meetings of the county were held in Walker's home in Calhoun, and he served as one of the county's first justices of the peace. The Walker name has remained intact across the years in the county.

An example of the European settlers in the county is the story of another Calhoun area family, the Sheltons, who trace their American lineage to a Ralph Shelton who was born in 1665 in Middlesex County, Virginia. Four generations later, Roderick Shelton served as a private in the Continental Army under George Washington. His son, James, moved to North Carolina in 1791; his son, James, at age 18 came to Greene County in Tennessee and married a Betsy Lawson. Around 1810 they loaded all of their belongings on a flatboat and floated down the Tennessee to the Hiwassee, and then traveled up the Hiwassee to a place on the McMinn side of the river across from the large Cherokee Village at present-day Charleston. Why they decided to stop at this particular point, or if they planned originally where their journey would take them, is not clear.

The Sheltons erected a log cabin, had a child, and soon thereafter Betsy died. James enlisted in the army, fought beside Sam

Houston at Horseshoe Bend, and was back in the area by 1816 when he married Sarah Hooper. They built a two-story frame house near the old log structure which became a well-known historical site until the TVA cleared the area in the late 1930s.

It should be repeated that the Walker and Shelton stories are not unique. They are representative of precisely the kinds of people, particularly of Cherokee and English, and later of Scotch-Irish descent, that would come to live together and populate McMinn County. The events that punctuate these family histories were undoubtedly repeated time and again among the first families that settled the county.

The United States has always been characterized by the great mobility of its people. The mass migration to the "Southwest Territory" in the early nineteenth century populated McMinn County and all of the lands to the Mississippi in this first stage of "Manifest Destiny." A traveling missionary, David McClure, described a typical family group as it moved into the new lands:

> The man carried an ax and gun, the wife the rim of a spinning wheel and a loaf of bread. Several little boys and girls, each with a bundle according to their size. Two poor horses, each heavily loaded. On the top of the baggage of one was an infant, rocked to sleep in a kind of wicker cage. A cow was one of the company, a bed-cord wound around her horns, and a bag of meal on her back.

During this same period families arrived whose descendants are still important in the county. Many came because they had either purchased land grants or secured them through military service. Many of these people were farmers; others followed as traders, merchants, or mill operators. It is impossible to do justice to this group here. Those mentioned are merely representative.

Asbury M. Coffey was the son of Eli Coffey who went into Kentucky with Daniel Boone. He lived in Athens until 1842 and was instrumental in some of the first railroading ventures in the county. He married Mary Bradford, the daughter of Colonel Henry Bradford who was a large landowner at the now-little-known settlement of Columbus which once existed in the southern part of the county and now is in Polk County. Coffey left Athens when President Millard Filmore appointed him to oversee Indian affairs in Kansas; later, one of his children migrated to Oregon.

Jesse Mayfield, whose family name is now carried forward by the Mayfield Dairy Farms, was born in New York in 1770. He secured several tracts of land that became available after the Hiwassee Purchase. One of the purchases, northeast of Athens, has never left the family. In fact, the original log home which Jesse Mayfield built was restored and stood as a county landmark on the property of his descendant Scott Mayfield until it was lost in a fire early in 1983.

One of the most significant contracting and building firms of the Tennessee frontier has close ties with McMinn County. In 1825 Samuel Clegg (after the Civil War the name was spelled "Cleage") settled in the Mouse Creek community. Clegg's father was from Pennsylvania, and had become very wealthy building mansions throughout that region in the late 1700s. The family can trace its lineage back to Belfast, Ireland.

With his son-in-law, Thomas Crutchfield, Clegg established the firm that came to be known as "Cleage and Crutchfield." With extensive help from slaves and using methods of brick laying that he had developed, Clegg contributed substantially to the architecture of East Tennessee. Several buildings in Athens were constructed by the firm, including the Mars Hill Presbyterian Church and the old Hiwassee Rail Road headquarters building which still stands on North Jackson Street. The grand courthouse which dominated the town square for the better part of the last century was built by Thomas and William Cleage in 1874. At one time the firm held contracts for nine courthouses in East Tennessee.

The Cantrell family has long been important in the eastern part of the county. John Cantrell, the first member of the Cantrell family in America, was from Pennsylvania and had both Huguenot and Quaker antecedents. Like many frontier families, the Cantrells had a large number of children: 21 sons and

Original architect's sketch for the county's first courthouse.

2 daughters, who contributed to proliferation of the clan from Pennsylvania to Georgia.

One family legend describes a time when John Cantrell went into a mercantile shop and asked to see hats for boys. The merchant displayed his selection of about a dozen hats, whereupon Cantrell stepped to the door and called his boys into the store. Twenty-one young men lined up at the counter, and the storekeeper was so flabbergasted that he gave each boy a new hat.

One old record asserted that "the common wealth of McMinn County has from pioneer days down revered the name of Cooke." In fact, the Cooke ancestry has crossed bloodlines with families as well-known as that of the English novelist Henry Fielding and the Tennessee senator Estes Kefauver. William Henry Cooke moved his family from South Carolina to McMinn County in 1820. He made large land purchases in the present Etowah area, operated an iron forge, and was a surveyor. He was active in laying out the town of Athens, was a state legislator, and helped start the State Bank of Athens. While serving as the institution's first president, he rode horseback every morning 13 miles to town and was always on the job by eight in the morning. Cooke was also active in the Meridian Sun Lodge No. 50, F&AM, which was always an important institution in the county. Cooke and his wife Mary had 12 children.

The court records of the first quarter century of the county's existence reveal a high reliance on the counsel and judgement of Charles Fleming Keith. In many respects he charted the course and established the strong foundation upon which the county rested for its first century. Keith had been born in Virginia in 1781 and by age eighteen was a law student with a close relative, Charles Marshall, who was a brother of the famous chief justice of the United States Supreme Court, John Marshall. By 1819 Keith was a practicing attorney in Jefferson County and actively involved in the early sessions of the Tennessee Legislature.

Following the Indian treaties of this period in which he took a large part, Keith came to McMinn County where he was a leader in every respect—political, civic, religious, and social. By 1850 he owned 15,000 acres of land, 44 slaves, and was the main taxpayer in the entire county. By the time of his death in 1857, Keith had performed the duties of a federal judge longer than any other American with the exception of Chief Justice Marshall himself. A large local Methodist church still carries the Keith name, and Mrs. Marshall Keith resides today in the stately Keith mansion which is the best-known residence in the county.

Other families, of no less significance than the representative examples noted here, have roots sunk deeply into the early history of America and eventually came to McMinn before or near the time of its inception. The sequicentennial edition of *The Daily Post-Athenian* detailed several, including the history of the Lane family, whose forebears, Isaac and Tidence Lane, came to the county in the early immigrations, constructed a mill from Tennessee-made brick, owned a large number of slaves, and finally left the area for lands in Mississippi that could produce more cotton. The Kimbrough and Carlock families gave substance to the religious growth of the region. Clement Vann Rogers, born ten miles south of Athens on the old W. C. Townsend place, was the father of American humorist Will Rogers. Other names are prominent in the *Post-Athenian* chronicle: Ballew, Barb, Boone, Burn, Cass, Cooper, Dorsey, Fisher, Fore, Gettys, Gilbreath, Guthrie, Hart, Hill, Hoyal, Lowry, Love, Matlock, Parkinson, Shipley, Smith, Snider, Sullins, and Wilkins.

Joseph McMinn, for whom the county was named, is an appropriate conclusion to this section. McMinn was born in Pennsylvania in 1758 and migrated into the area around 1775. He was active in the first political movements of the state and involved in the 1796 convention in Knoxville which drafted the proposed first constitution for the state. McMinn insisted that a "Bill of Rights" be included, and he personally carried the proposed constitution to President George Washington.

After serving in eight general assemblies and being speaker of the senate three times, McMinn was elected governor in 1815. He was reelected in 1817 and 1819. Although plagued by fiscal problems, McMinn's administrations dealt rather successfully with Indian problems, advanced education, and actively supported

Joseph McMinn, the three-time governor of Tennessee, for whom the county is named

improvement of river navigation. He is remembered as being quite popular with the general population.

In 1821 McMinn returned to farming in Rogersville, but by 1823 had accepted a position as agent to the Cherokees at Charleston's Fort Cass. He lived in Calhoun and served as agent until his sudden death, which occurred while he was writing at his desk on November 17, 1824. While in Calhoun, McMinn became a member of the Presbyterian Church and it was his desire to be buried in its graveyard.

In an interesting aside, the grave—like so many —went unmarked, and just one person, a Mr. R. J. M. Only, knew its location. When, in 1880, a plan was proposed to dig up the remains and take them to Athens for reburial and the erection of a "proper" monument, Mr. Only refused to show where the grave was. Only was an eccentric lay preacher who had supposedly read the Bible 27 times, argued his interpretations in all kinds of public settings, and was not beyond the convincing power of a good fist fight. He won the day and the monument was erected in the old Presbyterian cemetery at Calhoun where it stands in high visibility today.

The Cherokee Removal

Given the close relationship which existed between the English pioneers and the Cherokees, the integration of the races through intermarriage which by 1800 constituted a racial synthesis (the famous chief, John Ross, was only one-eighth Cherokee) in many areas like McMinn County, and the sophistication of the Cherokee people, the forced removal in the late 1830s of the majority of the tribe—which came to be known as the "Trail of Tears— is one of the darkest spots in the history of American expansion. McMinn County was in the center of the conflict, and the best evidence suggests that the citizenry of that time was strongly opposed to such inhumane and immoral activities. In fact, something of the "states' rights" sentiment that became of crucial importance in this area within a generation may have been born at this moment.

Stereotypes about primitive Indians wandering around half-naked must be set aside when considering the early nineteenth century Cherokees. These were people who were living a settled, civilized existence that paralleled in every way that of their white counterparts. By 1805 Return J. Meigs, for whom Meigs County was named and whose granddaughter married John Walker, Jr., was taking care of Indian matters in the area. First he operated from "Old Agency" in present-day Meigs County, and finally at the agency established across the Hiwassee from Calhoun at Charleston. Meigs attained a wide reputation for helping the Cherokees with farming, diversification of crops, raising of livestock, and trade.

Although large numbers of Cherokees had voluntarily left for new lands in the West, by 1828 the equally large number remaining continued to advance their own culture and strengthen their relationships with the white culture. In fact, one of the first successful American missionary activities was conducted in this area with the establishment of several mission schools which provided education for the Cherokee children. Probably more Cherokees were educated in the region at this time than whites.

But early in 1829 the entire picture changed. Gold was discovered on Cherokee land in Georgia near Dahlonoga! According to Kenneth Valliere in an article on Jackson for the *Tennessee Historical Quarterly*: "Between four and seven thousand gamblers, swindlers, debauchers, and profane blackguards, with morals as bad as it is to conceive, overran the Cherokee country."

The Georgia legislature immediately claimed all Cherokee land. With a singlemindedness that would have made the old Spanish conquistadors proud, Governor George Gilmer even decreed that the land would be given to whites by lottery if the Cherokees could be removed. The tenor of the conflict soon assumed national significance. Andrew Jackson, who had commanded the Cherokees at Horseshoe Bend, had become president in 1829. The Cherokee chiefs, thinking they had a sure friend in Jackson, appealed for consideration. Hard-nosed political pragmatist to the end, Jackson supported the position of Georgia.

The Cherokees then went to Washington and appealed to the Supreme Court and John Marshall—perhaps given quick entrance because of the chief justice's relationship with the Keith family. The strongest supporter of the Cherokee claim was the Tennessee congressman, Davy Crockett. Crockett poked cutting sarcasm at the whole idea of removal of the Cherokees by introducing a bill calling for the removal of the white residents of East Tennessee to the West, "lest they impede the territorial designs and sovereignty of the State of Georgia." In fact, in 1832, the Supreme Court ruled in favor of the Cherokees. Cartter Patten recalls in *A Tennessee Chronicle* that the high court ruled: "The Cherokee Nation is a distinct community, occupying its own territory, in which the laws of Georgia can have no force." There was great rejoicing in the Cherokee Nation, but the Cherokees did not know of President Jackson's reputed remark: "John Marshall has made his decision, now let him enforce it."

Even the Cherokees were set at odds with each other. This internal division had a direct impact on McMinn County when in 1834 John Walker, Jr., who was also known as "Chief Jack," was murdered by fellow-Cherokee James Foreman after Walker had undertaken what Foreman considered unauthorized negotiations in Washington involving treaties that would lead to removal.

Foreman, with an accomplice named Isaac Springston, came to trial in Athens, but soon the question of murder became secondary to the question of jurisdiction. Being quite sensitive to their environment, the McMinn jurors concluded that the matter was wholly Cherokee and that they had all rights to adjudicate the case. However, as part of their desire to have higher claim on the Indians, the United States government got the McMinn decision reversed.

While the Cherokees met to raise money for yet another appeal to the Supreme Court, Foreman and Springston, in some manner not a matter of record, suddenly were no longer to be found in the Athens jail. It seems that "frontier justice" prevailed, and that McMinn Countians found a subtle way of overruling the United States and affirming the stand that they took throughout the controversy. Records indicate that Foreman went West, was actively involved in seeking out and killing those who had agreed with the removal among his own people, and was eventually killed himself.

Jackson sent the Reverend J. F. Schermerhorn into the area; he obtained highly questionable treaties from impressionable splinter groups who were generally unauthorized by the tribe as a whole and their central leader, Chief John Ross of Chattanooga. Schermerhorn was not beyond using whiskey and individual bribes to get the treaties that were ultimately accepted by the federal government and enforced by General Winfield Scott and 7000 troops beginning in May of 1838.

The Cherokees were corralled by the hundreds at Charleston, Ross' Landing/Chattanooga, and Guntersville, Alabama.

Citizens of McMinn petitioned for an end to the roundup, but no relief was forthcoming. An unidentified local missionary reported in his journal:

> The Cherokees are nearly all prisoners. They are dragged from their houses and encamped in military places all over the area. They are allowed no time to take with them anything except the clothes they have on. Well furnished houses are left prey to plunderers who, like hungry wolves, follow in the train of the captors. These wretches rifle the houses, and strip the helpless, unoffending owners of all they have on earth.

The following advertisement was placed in regional newspapers by Joseph Harris, disbursing agent for the Cherokee Removal under the heading "Wagons Wanted":

> Sixteen first rate road wagons with bodies of the largest kinds, each to be drawn by first rate six horse teams complete in gear and harness, will find employment during the removal of the present Emigration of Cherokees from their homes to their respective points; by their owners of such enrolling their names immediately at the agency.
>
> Three dollars and fifty cents per day will be allowed as a full compensation for the services of each team and its appertenances so employed—a loaded team to travel fifteen miles per day, without a load twenty miles. All ferriages excepting over the Hiwassee to be government charges.

Before the deportation was complete, nearly 5000 Cherokees had died, many from cold and hunger. Perhaps a thousand escaped to find refuge in the Tennessee and western North Carolina mountains. The will of the federal government ultimately triumphed, and a major segment of McMinn County's unique culture was destroyed.

From the Cherokee Removal to the Civil War

The period from the Cherokee Removal to the Civil War was a time of great growth in the county. Individuals emerged who would make lasting contributions. Finally, people began to stay rather than move on to the new frontiers. The fixtures of civilization—schools, churches, and political systems—could now be given lasting foundations.

Those present at the organizational meeting of the county on November 13, 1819, at the home of John Walker in Calhoun were Archibald Black, Hambright Black, George Colville, Samuel Dickey, Benjamin Griffith, Jacob Sharp, and Walker. The first elected officials were Young Colville, clerk; Spencer Beavers, sheriff; A. R. Turk, trustee; Benjamin Hambright, registrar; Griffith Dickeson, ranger; and Jacob Work, coroner. Charles Fleming Keith organized the first court in 1820. Goodspeed's *History of East Tennessee (1887)* says of Keith that "He was a quiet, unassuming man, of sound judgement, and had a good knowledge of the law; his decisions were rarely reversed by the supreme court."

The first settlers of the county's first town, Calhoun, were the Colvilles, John Cowan, Benjamin Hambright, E. P. Owen, Eli Sharp, and A. R. Turk. A Presbyterian church was erected in 1823. In this same year Martin Cassidy at Cedar Springs was asked to donate land for a new county seat that would be centrally located—he refused. Land was donated at Athens for this purpose by William Lowry.

Specific reports about life in the county between 1834 and 1852 are difficult to find. The 1834 edition of the *Tennessee Gazetteer* claimed a total population of 14,497: 6732 "free white males," 6487 "free white females," 21 "free colors," and 1257 slaves. Athens, always the most populous community, had a population of about 500 at that time. Most professions, businesses, and educational institutions of that time are represented in the *Gazetteer's* description of the city.

New settlers named Fyffe and Smith operated the first stores in Athens. Other early merchants were Solomon Bogart, Francis Boyd, John Crawford, Alexander and David Cleage, George Morgan, and O. G. Murrell. Joel Brown owned a tailor shop, and Peter Kinder, a hattery. There were a silversmith, George Sehorn, and a coppersmith, Julius Blackwell. Demsey Casey owned a saddlery, while James Gettys and Squire Johnson operated a tannery.

The first doctors were John Farmer, Horace Hickox, Samuel Jordan, and Benjamin Stout. The first attorneys were Thomas Campbell, Spencer Jarnagin (who served in Congress under James K. Polk), and Return J. Meigs. Campbell achieved statewide acclaim, as did T. Nixon Van Dyke, who located in Athens in 1829. In 1835 a branch of the Planter's Bank was opened, and in 1838 a branch of the State Bank. The first church, Zion Hill, was built by the Baptists.

By 1850, Goodspeed reported, "Athens was at the height of its prosperity." Important businesses included: William Ballew; William Burns; A. Clèage and Company; Grubb and Engledow; J. M. Henderson; George Horne; King and Crutchfield; McEwin and Gillespie; John McGaughey; A. McKeldin; Moss and Jackson; J. K. Reeder; Robeson, Sartain and Company; George Ross; Sehorn and Hornsby; and W. C. Witt and Company. C. Zimmerman established a foundry about 1852, and the Methodist Episcopal female college was enjoying a growing reputation.

Smaller communities developed as railroads came into the county. Riceville (on land donated by Charles W. Rice), Sanford, and Mouse Creek (Niota) all started as sites of railroad stations and soon attracted small businesses and homes. Mouse Creek was particularly prosperous. J. H. Magill opened the first store there in 1855. Other merchants in the area, according to Goodspeed, were E. Cate, J. N. Dalzell, A. Forrest, and Stephens & Browder. Early settlers at Mouse Creek included Greenbury Cate, L. R. Hurst, J. L. Hurst, John F. Sherman, H. L. Shultz, and James Willson. Many of the descendants of these people remain important in the northern part of the county.

The Coming of War

The years immediately preceeding the Civil War were a time of great drama for the nation. However, the war was uniquely accentuated in East Tennessee and in counties like McMinn. It is, of course, common knowledge that the proverbial "brother

The remains of the Gettys Mill on the Eastanallee near Sanford

against brother" division of loyalties between North and South occurred throughout this area more often than perhaps any place in the entire nation. It took years to relax hard and fast political lines that had been drawn between "secessionists" and "Unionists" in early 1860. McMinn County played a unique role in these activities.

Before that uniqueness is explored, one common misconception must be cleared up. It is often thought that the major issue dividing Tennessee was slavery, and that East Tennessee had fewer large farms and therefore less need for slaves than Middle and West Tennessee. There is information to undergird this view, and undoubtedly it did play at least some role. In 1840 there were only 19,915 slaves in East Tennessee; this number increased to only 27,500 by 1860. Comparable figures in Middle Tennessee show an increase from 106,640 to 148,000, and in West Tennessee an increase from 56,600 to 100,200.

By 1860 East Tennessee had only 10 percent of the state's slave population and only 9 percent of the population of the region was slave. These numbers are quite small compared to the other major divisions of the state. McMinn County in 1860 had 124 slaveholders who owned 678 slaves. As early statistics indicate, this number had decreased by almost 50 percent since 1834.

However, East Tennessee can in no way be construed as a hotbed of abolitionist sentiment. Most of the strong Unionists were slaveholders. Abolitionist movements like the one at Maryville College in nearby Blount County were not well received. There is at least one account of abolitionist tracts coming to the Athens post office and being turned over by the postmaster to people in the streets who burned them.

The dominant idea seemed to be that slavery could continue, and that the lot of the slave could be improved and protected by law. Paul Bergeron reports on two interesting cases in this regard. In one, a slave convicted of rape by a lower court was acquitted by the state supreme court, and the lower court was severely criticized for misconduct. In the second, a Washington County man willed his 112 acre farm to slaves, rather than his seven sons, and gave the slaves their freedom. When the sons sued, the courts upheld the claim of the slaves. One state supreme court decision, quoted by Bergeron, read:

> The law takes the slave out of the hands of the master and treats the slave as a rational and intelligent human being, responsible to moral, social, and municipal duties and obligations, and gives him the benefit of all the forms of trial which jealousy of power and love of liberty have induced the free man to throw around himself for his own protection.

This middle-of-the-road policy was probably more appealing to McMinn Countians. In fact, they may originally have had a perspective on this issue that was even more liberal. In 1834 a new state constitution was drafted. A gradual emancipation provision was introduced and supported by the signatures of 1800 leading citizens from 16 counties—McMinn was one of them. Eventually the constitutional convention, by a vote of 44 to 10, disallowed the provision. The McMinn delegation cast one of the 10 supporting votes.

By the 1850s the emancipation position was essentially over. Secessionists painted the northern abolitionists as meddlers and demagogues who would like nothing better than to start infringing upon the privacy of internal state matters. The challenging issue had become state's rights. Abraham Lincoln was seen as a frighteningly malicious usurper of independence. Secessionists created an exaggerated image of abolitionists much like Joseph McCarthy created of communists a hundred years later.

Strict Unionists held doggedly to their positions out of a deep-seated sense of loyalty. Their ancestors had fought and died for this Union at King's Mountain and Horsehoe Bend. They were convinced that without strong centralization no government could endure, and they understood the consequences of a civil war. They were disciples of Henry Clay and Daniel Webster, and largely disdained John Calhoun's state's rights views—Calhoun had been too dictatorial for many, especially in McMinn County, in some of his dealings with the Indians.

Unfortunately, the march of events quickened. On December 20, 1860, the "Convention of South Carolina" passed what was termed with great fanfare an "Ordinance of Secession." Hastily, to preserve some presence in the area, the United States Army took control of an antiquated harbor garrison, Fort Sumter—the lines of inevitable conflict were drawn.

Other southern leaders called for similar conventions, and none was louder than Governor Isham G. Harris of Tennessee. Harris had been actively involved in the 1860 presidential campaign of John C. Breckenridge, who held the most extreme southern views. Early in January of 1861 Harris convened the Tennessee General Assembly and with a fusillade of disdain proclaimed vengeance against the Unionist position. He called for a vote on February 9 to determine whether Tennessee would have its own convention to discuss secession.

One could have easily predicted, by looking at the election returns in 1860, the quandary in which McMinn Countians would find themselves. Breckenridge had failed to carry Tennessee, being defeated by the Whig/Consitutional Union candidate John Bell in a vote of 69,176 to 64,809. In East Tennessee, that vote had been 22,043 to 18,800, and in McMinn County 986 to 978—the closest race in the entire state. Bell had strong Union loyalty at the time of the election, but it must also be recalled that he was a native Tennessean in the race.

There commenced one of the most memorable times in the state's history, and especially in the swing area of East Tennessee. The East Tennessee and Georgia Railroad cut across the western section of the county, and had major stations at Niota, Athens, and Riceville. Some of the most powerful political voices in the nation came to East Tennessee on the railroad. Speeches that went on for hours were typical. The Unionist leaders were men of such high status as Andrew Johnson (then a senator, but vice-president four years later), Horace Maynard, T. A. R. Nelson, O. P. Temple, and C. F. Trigg.

The secessionist leaders, in addition to Governor Harris, were equally commanding in their presence: John Crozier, Thomas Lyon, William Sneed, William Swan, Campbell Wallace, and William Yancy. Wallace was the president of the railroad which until 1855 had been headquartered in Athens—his was a familiar face throughout the county. The train depots and the courthouse square were scenes of continual rhetoric and debate. Occasionally there were threats, fist fights, and even gunfire as the voting day came closer.

The total vote in the referendum of February 9 was a mere 54.5 percent against the convention, but in East Tennessee it was 81 percent against. In McMinn County the vote was 439 for and 1457 against. Memphis and Nashville continued as centers of Confederate support, Memphians at one time discussing their own, private secession. Knoxville and Greeneville were centers of Unionist sentiment. Governor Harris continued, undaunted, in his desire to bring the state into the Confederacy.

Lincoln took office in March of 1861 and then ordered relief for the beseiged Fort Sumter in early April. On April 12 the Confederate forces fired on Sumter, and Lincoln responded by calling for 75,000 volunteers to rise to the defense of the Union. In less than two weeks, Harris reconvened the General Assembly and a second vote on separation was planned for June 8.

The speech-making began again with a greater intensity. Now Confederate soldiers in uniform were gallantly paraded before impassioned youth, and the specter of 75,000 northern soldiers pouring through Cumberland Gap was raised again and again.

Even John Bell, the stalwart Whig, finally succumbed to secessionist pressure to take up its cause. In a speech at Athens in early June he spoke half-heartedly about secession and then turned apologetically to his Unionist friend from McMinn County, John McGaughey, and said: "There is my friend, Mr. McGaughey, between whom and myself there used to be no difference in our view. I know not how he stands in reference to these new questions." McGaughey replied in his gentle, earnest voice: "I am still for the Union, the Constitution, and the enforcement of the laws." Many shared McGaughey's sentiments, in spite of the escalation of events. On May 30 the "East Tennessee Convention" was held in Knoxville to support the Union cause. McMinn County had 24 delegates; one of them, Dr. M. R. May, was chosen one of the vice-presidents. George Bridges was appointed to a reporting committee which produced a scalding indictment of the state legislature for its drift toward the Confederate cause.

In the referendum of June 8, Middle and West Tennessee voted overwhelmingly for seccession, while East Tennessee voted more than two to one to remain in the Union. In McMinn County the vote was 904 for seccession and 1,144 against. With the majority of McMinn County and East Tennessee remaining loyal, there was a final effort; a Unionist convention was held at Greeneville on June 17 to protest severe voting irregularities. The document prepared by this convention was dramatic, a profound political treatise in the finest of the American tradition. Unfortunately, the Greenveville convention was ineffectual—the die was cast. The McMinn delegates to this convention were M. D. Anderson, G. W. Bridges, A. C. Derrick, and John McGaughey.

The most striking Unionist spokesman, however, has not been discussed and it is this personality that provides the focal point of McMinn County's unique contribution to this period. The setting for the appearance of the spokesman was the old Methodist Episcopal campground two miles south of Athens at Cedar Springs. In his memoirs Dr. David Sullins, who was born in Athens in 1827, described the campground and the events that transpired there:

> There was a small log church, and a shed one hundred feet long and twenty-five feet wide, with wings on hinges. When these wings were down, it was a great tent, and when they were up, it would seat two thousand. The tents were rude shacks made of logs, some still with the bark on. There were no fireplaces. Beds were scaffolds along the sides of the tents. All floors were dirt, covered with straw. At daybreak each morning, a loud horn sounded, at which time all arose and prepared for the day. Service hours were at 9:30 a.m., 11:00 a.m., 3:00 p.m., and "candle-lighting."

Into this scene stepped William G. "Parson" Brownlow, who was the minister of the Methodist Episcopal Church, South, in Athens, the forerunner of the present Keith Memorial United Methodist Church.

Brownlow was described as stepping into the pulpit, removing his gunbelt and pistol, and preaching "hell-fire and brimstone." The parson eventually led the Unionist movement in East Tennessee as editor of *The Knoxville Whig*. He spent most of the war years speaking in the North, hiding in Knoxville, and a short time in a Confederate prison. His wife was forced to move North, and his son was arrested for possessing and circulating an outlawed book, *Impending Crisis in the South*. Typical of the division that was occurring, the charges against the younger Brownlow were brought by Gen. James T. Lane of McMinn County.

Following one imprisonment and an eventual escape to safety behind Union lines in March of 1862 Brownlow proclaimed: "Glory to God in the highest, and on earth peace, good will towards men, except for a few hell-bent and hell-bound rebels in Knoxville." This was indicative of Brownlow's style. He was always on the attack. He had once written defiantly in *The Whig*:

> I have been expected to state in every issue of my paper, that the

mantle of Washington sits well on Jeff Davis! This would be a funny publication. The bow of Ulysses in the hands of a pygmy! The robes of a giant adorning Tom Thumb! The curls of Hyperion on the brow of a Satyr! The Aurora Borealis on a cotton farm melting down the icy North! This would be to metamorphose a minnow into a WHALE!

"Parson" Brownlow served as the first postwar governor of Tennessee. He was successful in introducing black suffrage in the state, and moved with deliberation to get Tennessee back into the Union—it was the first state to be readmitted. In 1869, after reelection and the strong opposition of Nathan Bedford Forrest's Ku Klux Klan with its desire to enfranchise ex-Confederates, Brownlow resigned to become a United States senator.

Brownlow was succeeded by DeWitt C. Senter from McMinn County. Senter alleviated tensions by reestablishing civil rather than military courts and by advancing the cause of Confederate suffrage. Senter was successful enough that the Ku Klux Klan was ordered by its Grand Wizard to destroy its robes and disband. Because of his quick conciliatory actions, reconstruction in Tennessee did not go through the same kind of painful experiences common in most of the south.

The Civil War

Immediately following the events at Fort Sumter, frenzied activity began. In fact, Governor Harris probably had already executed a series of pacts with the Confederate leaders and had been actively recruiting soldiers in Middle and West Tennessee. Although most Tennesseans wore the Confederate gray, at least 35,000 East Tennesseans joined the Union forces.

The Confederacy would have profited greatly if the people of East Tennessee had come solidly into line. Because they did not, the South lost a large number of dedicated fighting men. It also had to contend with the continual victimization of a major north-south thoroughfare by secret agents, guerrillas, and—at the very minimum—many unfriendly farmers and merchants, whose daily harassment and inconvenience impeded the practical movements of large masses of men. Some estimates have been made that, at any one time, between eight and ten thousand Confederate troops had to be kept in East Tennessee to manage public dissent. McMinn County, with perhaps a small majority of its own citizens in gray, was typical of the prevailing Union sentiment of East Tennessee.

Fighting forces began to organize into infantry, cavalry, and artillery units. Sometimes units were organized over wide geographical areas, but most fighting units were organized by local men who appealed to their friends and neighbors. In this way, it was not unusual for lifelong friends and relatives to fight together throughout the war. Union companies, however, were not actually formed in the county until late in the war when its outcome was fairly well assured.

Eight important Confederate units were specifically formed from within the county. Company A of the 3rd (Brazelton's) Tennessee Cavalry Battalion was organized on August 3, 1861, with James C. Bradford as major and J. A. Gouldy as captain. One of their first assignments was to go into Clay County, Kentucky, to a salt mine and get two hundred barrels of salt. In some respects, salt was as important to an army as bullets. This unit fought at the Battle of Fishing Creek, and was active later in the war throughout the Cumberland Gap area. Company B of the 16th Tennessee Cavalry Battalion was organized at Athens on May 31, 1862, under the leadership of John R. Neal and E. W. Rucker, but little is known about this unit's activities.

Company I of the 1st (Roger's) East Tennessee Cavalry Regiment was also organized within the county. The unit had a beleaguered and lackluster war record which prompted Gen. Kirby Smith officially to record his belief that the large number of Union friends and relatives which members of this unit had rendered them ineffective in carrying out the demands of combat. One wonders if such a feeling might not have prevailed among many of the soldiers from the county.

Willie Lowry and W. P. H. McDermott organized Company H of the 19th Tennessee Infantry Regiment. First fighting at Fishing Creek, the unit then faced major action at Vicksburg.

There they attempted a surprise attack through almost impenetrable swamps. The suspected Union force turned out to be a hoax, but a major part of the regiment was lost or rendered ineffective by the terrible conditions. The unit suffered 94 casualities out of a little over two hundred men at Chickamauga, but was still able to have said about it at Missionary Ridge and the retreat toward Atlanta: "The 19th was never once driven from any position to which it was assigned." After fighting in almost every major battle of the Army of Tennessee, only 64 men were left at the time of the surrender at Appomatox.

Three other units also saw major action at Vicksburg. Company F of the 39th (W. M. Bradford's) Tennessee Infantry Regiment, which was mustered at Mouse Creek on March 17, 1862, under Albartus Forrest and John C. Neil, twice took pleasure boats fitted with cannon and captured Union gunboats. At the end of the war, this unit was acting as a protective escort for Jefferson Davis. Company H of the 43rd Tennessee Infantry Regiment, which was organized at Riceville on November 16, 1861, fought with Jubal Early, participated in his raid on Washington in 1864, and counted 972 holes in its unit flag at Vicksburg. Finally, three local companies, A, H, and K, of the 59th Tennessee Infantry Regiment, under James B. Cooke and John M. Van Dyke were described in official communications following Vicksburg: "During these 47 days, under the terrific fire of the enemy's artillery and infantry, the officers and men bore themselves with constancy and courage. Often half-fed, and ill-clothed, exposed to the burning sun and soaking rain, they performed their duty cheerfully and without murmur."

Twelve Union companies were formed in the county and assigned to four different regiments. It should also be remembered that many from the county who fought for the Union did so by going North and joining forces from other areas. While the activities of the six companies of the 7th Tennessee Mounted Infantry Regiment will be detailed later, some mention of the activities of the other units has found its way into official war records.

Company M of the 9th Tennessee Cavalry Regiment was

mustered in Nashville on June 28, 1864. At one time in 1865 the unit was ordered to take and execute prisoners, especially if it was determined that they were guerrillas and bushwackers. Evidence suggests that, since they were operating in their own territory, they refused to carry out the orders with the severity commanded.

Companies C, D, and I of the 10th Tennessee Cavalry Regiment saw extensive action in Middle Tennessee, especially against Generals "Fighting Joe" Wheeler and Nathan Bedford Forrest. At one time they were in the saddle for eight days and nights against Forrest and traveled over two hundred miles fighting one skirmish after another. Finally, Companies A and D of the 5th Tennessee Mounted Infantry Regiment, which was mustered at Riceville, Calhoun, Cleveland, and Athens in October and November of 1864 under Spencer Boyd and James S. Bradford, saw limited action during the latter part of the war in northern Georgia.

These units were engaged in a multitude of major conflicts and a continual series of smaller skirmishes. McMinn Countians were present at Shiloh, Manassas, Vicksburg, Chickamauga, Missionary Ridge, and Knoxville. They faced the finest generals and bravest troops on both sides of the conflict. The records speak of deaths, wounds, imprisonments, exchanges, and returns home.

No major battles occurred in the county itself. At most there were small skirmishes that received little notice in the official reports. There were gun emplacements and bunkers on Depot Hill in Athens to protect the railroad station, and there is some indication that fights occurred at this spot from time to time as the town changed hands many times during the war.

To assume from the absence of major battles that the county was relatively untouched by the war would be misleading. The cataclysmic impact that a movement of ten to twenty thousand troops through an area would have is hard to imagine. In addition, fighting did not generally take place during the winter months and an entire region could become responsible for "wintering" troops. The strain on the already meager food supplies and shelter was phenomenal. McMinn County was at the heart of these kinds of activities, involving both Northern and Southern armies, throughout the course of the war.

Farmlands were ravaged, fences destroyed, spoils were taken on both sides, and individual fortunes that had been established since the first settlement were steadily depleted. The presence of the railroad line insured this, and concerns about protection or disruption of vital rail services kept troops in the area. In addition, lawless hoodlums, termed "bushwackers," used the disorganization of the war to carry out personal vendettas, plundering Unionist and Confederate alike. One of the worst of this type, a man named John P. Gatewood, was christened in legend "The Red-headed Beast from Georgia," and operated with a band of fifty Confederate deserters in this immediate area.

The region was not burned over like Atlanta and southeastern Georgia. In fact, Gen. William T. Sherman himself operated from the county for a period after the battles at Chattanooga and Knoxville and before his march to the sea. He used the Bridges Hotel in Athens as his headquarters and seemed to develop some real affection for the town. After the war the area was left drained and poor, and "reconstruction" would have to mean much more than political reorganization.

The Van Dyke mansion, which still stands on the Maxwell White property overlooking Cedar Grove Cemetery, was also used by Sherman. This would have been the highest insult for the property's owner, T. Nixon Van Dyke, who was the staunchest of Southerners. Van Dyke was an important judge, a central figure in the government of the Confederacy, and was imprisoned along with his wife for several years following the war. He refused to ask for a pardon and was freed only after other members of his family sought the intervention of President Andrew Johnson. Van Dyke, who refused to shave until the full independence of the Confederacy could be attained, is remembered as having a beard that finally had to be hung back across his shoulders.

When Sherman arrived, he found the home occupied only by a group of women, all their husbands being off fighting in the Southern cause. He felt that Athens was no fit place for women

The Van Dyke mansion, where Sherman stayed during the Civil War

who were alone under the present circumstances of war and issued passes that allowed for passage through Northern lines to the home of kinfolk in Quincy, Illinois.

Earlier in the war, a campfire had been spotted late one evening on the hill at the top of the cemetery. Mrs. William Deaderick Van Dyke climbed the hill to inquire about which army the soldiers represented. The reply that came back through the dim light: "Colonel Nathan Bedford Forrest, ma'am, at your service."

Several examples can be given to help recall what daily challenges the citizenry faced during the war. Protecting belongings, particularly horses and cattle, from the armies was a major problem. My grandfather recalled that every time an army came near, he, a child of eight or nine years, was given the responsibility of taking the family mule to a hiding place that had been cut out in a nearby canebreak. This Moses-in-the-bullrushes tactic preserved something that may have been much more essential to the lives of the general population than any ideological allegiances.

On a larger scale, the Wattenbargers who had a reputation as fine merchants of North Athens in later years, were known for their excellent stock breeding and trading during the war era. Legend has it that the family hit upon the tactic of keeping the best stock well-hidden and a blind mule and an old horse with a plaster patch on its back on public display. Soldiers would be told that this was all that was left of the stock, and that, in fact, the horse had a "strange infection" that they were having to treat. Usually the soldiers did not stay around long to ask further questions.

Not everybody tried to keep their stock from the military. Some of the finest cavalry horses used in the Civil War were foaled on the farm of the James T. Lane family of McMinn County. One particular unit, known as "Lane's Guards" and fighting as part of the First Tennessee Cavalry, CSA, carried combat banners sewn by Athens ladies.

There was also the problem of noncombatants being "drafted" by armies as they moved through an area. Joe Hughes was a Unionist living in the Clearwater area. He had avoided conscription, like many in the area, to remain at home to care for crops and to protect his family. A large Confederate force moved from Kingston to Athens along the Old Kingston Road near his home and came too close. Hughes and two friends named Culvahouse and Woods decided that they could stay no longer. They walked to the Tennessee River in Meigs County, swam the river, and enlisted in the First Cavalry Company, USA, which was at the time camping in the region.

The practice of "wintering" could bring large numbers of soldiers and commanders. For example, the Union army camped at Athens in the winter of 1863, using the nearly-completed Keith mansion as headquarters. The commander carefully gave the influential Keiths receipts for any item his men used. Small log huts housing eight men each called "tents" were built throughout the present Epperson/Athens Community Hospital area. There were hundreds of these small buildings.

The building called "Old College" in the heart of the present

"Old College" on the Tennessee Wesleyan campus, which served as a hospital during the Civil War and now houses the McMinn County Historical Museum

Tennessee Wesleyan College campus, which now houses the McMinn County Living Heritage Museum, was used as a Confederate hospital at one time during the war. Churches, academy buildings, and homes were regularly used to quarter troops; occasionally one army would burn a building when it left so the approaching army could not use it.

The most notable events of the war related to the Hiwassee River Bridge at Calhoun. In fact, one of the first major events of the entire war occurred here. Federal forces realized that the river and rail systems in Tennessee were essential to any advances by either army, and that the destruction of this bridge and several others like it—in much the way that Andrews' Raiders would do in the "Great Locomotive Chase" in North Georgia later in the war—should be given high priority in any war plans.

Lincoln himself was reported to have said that the destruction of the East Tennessee railroad system, particularly the bridge over the Tennessee at Loudon and the bridge at Calhoun, was as important as the capture of Richmond itself. By mid-fall 1861 he and Gen. George McClellan had approved the clandestine plan of Presbyterian minister William Carter to burn nine bridges in East Tennessee on the night of November 8, 1861. McClellan planned a major thrust into East Tennessee immediately following the completion of this mission to quickly control the area.

While the guerrillas hid in the mountains and completed their plans, McClellan changed his mind at the insistence of Gen. Don Carlos Buell, who wanted to attack Middle Tennessee. Unaware of this, attempts at bridge destruction were carried out at several locations including the Hiwassee bridge. This group was led by A. M. Cate who lived in Bradley County, but had strong family ties in McMinn. Accompanying Cate were Thomas Cate, Eli Cleveland, Jesse F. Cleveland, and Adam Thomas. A. M. Cate had to walk 300 miles through the Tennessee mountains to escape into Kentucky and avoid the reign of terror which followed the burnings.

Great fear spread throughout the state's population, martial law was instituted, dozens of people were arrested daily for several weeks, and there were several immediate executions. Many who were guilty of little more than fostering Union sympathies were marched off in the dead of winter to prisons in Georgia and Alabama. The Union plan had not taken into consideration the southerners' ability to rebuild and repair—the Hiwassee Bridge was operational within two weeks of the burning. In fact, the bridge burnings may have worked to the advantage of the South, as many people who had been undecided were frightened and joined the Confederate cause as the realities of war struck so close to their homes.

The bridge was the site of a number of battles and skirmishes throughout the war. One major confrontation involved commands led by Gen. James Longstreet and General Sherman in the fall of 1863. To delay Sherman, Longstreet set fire to the bridge, which necessitated a river crossing. With Longstreet holding the high ground overlooking the river, Sherman's crossing became a deadly affair. He stood on the river bank and cried out, "Recollect that East Tennessee is my horror."

Following the Battle of Chickamauga, a second, major engagement involved forces under Nathan Bedford Forrest against Gen. Ambrose Burnside. Forrest paid dearly for a momentary success against Burnside and shifted his attention to Middle and West Tennessee for the remainder of the war. Finally, following the Battle of Fort Sanders at Knoxville, Gen. "Fighting Joe" Wheeler led 1500 men against Union Col. Eli Long, who was encamped near the bridge. Many of Wheeler's men advanced in a valiant saber charge and fought hand to hand. Long's superior troops were, however, victorious, and the last vestige of Confederate strength in Tennessee was broken.

While all of the events of the Civil War that involved McMinn Countians cannot be recounted, at least the activities of two representative units—one Confederate and one Union—can be examined closely.

Col. John C. Vaughn's regiment, organized in Knoxville on May 29, 1861, became the third Tennessee group to be accepted into Confederate service. Assisting Vaughn was Col. Newton J. Lillard from Meigs County. The company mustered in McMinn County was led by Capt. Harry Dill. The formation of this unit afforded many young men from the county their first real opportunity to join the Southern cause.

The unit immediately left for the battlefront in Virginia, and, following several successful skirmishes, was involved in the First Battle of Manassas Junction in mid-July. Throughout the early part of 1862 the unit fought under Gen. Kirby Smith, and concentrated their efforts in upper East Tennessee in the pursuit of guerrilla forces and bushwackers. Their next engagement was at Tazewell in early August against three Union regiments. Although outnumbered, the Tennessee forces were victorious in the battle. Following further successes at Cumberland Gap, Vaughn was promoted to the rank of general and Lillard commanded the regiment until the end of the war.

About this time Gen. U. S. Grant began to move against

Vicksburg, and several East Tennessee units were ordered there. They faced Grant's superior numbers at the bloody battle at Baker's Creek and, of 3800 who fought in this valiant attempt to secure the city from further attack, only 2000 returned to the trenches at Vicksburg. For the 44 days of the seige the unit was responsible for successfully holding three hill batteries.

Following the surrender at Vicksburg, a period of internment, and subsequent exchange, Lillard reorganized Company G in Charleston in early October. At this time they were upgraded to mounted infantry, and joined the forces of General Longstreet to fight at Knoxville. With the exception of the surrender at Vicksburg, this was actually the first time that they had been unsuccessful in pitched battle. From this moment on, the war became treacherous, as an except from a war diary quoted by Wilma Dykeman shows:

> We were so badly off for horse-shoes that on the advance we had stripped the shoes from all the dead horses, and we killed for that purpose all the wounded and broken-down animals. During the siege the river brought down to us a number of dead horses and mules, thrown from the town. We watched for them, took them out, and got the shoes and nails from their feet. Our men were nearly as badly off as the animals—perhaps worse, as they did not have hoofs. I have seen bloody stains on frozen ground, left by the bare-footed where our infantry had passed. For shoes, we were obliged to resort to the raw hides of beef cattle as temporary protection from the frozen ground.

Further fighting in the Shenandoah Valley and upper East Tennessee continued in the final months of the war. There were a few victories but many disasters. Company G's fighting spirit never dwindled, and while Lee was bringing the conflict to an end at Appomatox, they were camped nearby at New River ready to take up the fight when so commanded. Lillard's own unit, in forced retreat and thinned by desertions, surrendered at Washington, Georgia, on May 9, 1865.

In the latter part of the war, five companies of men were mustered at Athens as the 7th Tennessee Mounted Infantry Regiment, USA. The regiment was stationed at Athens under the command of Majors John McGaughey and Oliver M. Dodson. Official records indicate that this unit participated only in the skirmish in Athens on January 29, 1865. George W. Ross, quartermaster of the unit, described the action:

> We were attacked yesterday by 300 rebels of Vaughn's, Wheeler's, and bushwacker commands, and repulsed them from the town, but they captured some 20 or 25 of our men, including major John McGaughey. They retreated from the town in the evening and remained all night seven miles from here, and rumor says they are going to make another attack in connection with about the same force that came from Madisonville yesterday.

An urgent request was sent to Knoxville for reinforcements, especially artillery units. The next afternoon, veteran soldiers arrived from Knoxville, and a somewhat different view of the situation was reported in the Civil War Centennial materials:

> The garrison of about 500 men were scattered through the town and the county, a greater portion of them having disappeared in the timber on the approach of the enemy the day previously and had not yet returned. From the best information, we have learned that about 200 guerrillas dashed into the place the day before about 1:00 P.M., and that they were in the public square before the garrison knew it; that they remained three hours, and drew off at their leisure without doing any injury to the town.

In March part of the regiment was ordered into the mountains east of Athens to patrol and guard the passes, and another group was sent to Clinton to help with martial law policing activities. Those who remained with the regiment were mustered out on July 27, 1865.

In many respects, primary source materials from this period are almost nonexistent. To follow regiments is one thing, but to know the individual acts of gallantry and ultimate sacrifice is quite another. Beyond the regimental histories, countless individuals, for one reason or another, fought in dozens of other units that were mustered in places far removed from McMinn County; their stories have not even been touched. The frontline combat of the Civil War was horrific, and in addition to the outright battle deaths thousands upon thousands died from infection, disease, starvation, and weather. The scars that remained were deep, and influenced political, family, and community differences over the next century.

In spite of the scars, oneness of place and future brought about a peaceful and productive postwar coexistence. The words of the chronicler of Vaughn's Brigade speak well of the Confederate spirit in defeat:

> The laying down of their arms, the striking of their colors, the disbanding of their military organizations, and the return of allegiance to the Federal Govenment, were not the choice of these long-tried veterans so long as there was hope; but when their bugles were silent, their flag in the dust, their campfires gone out, and their oath of fidelity to the South cancelled by the issues of war, they were ready to resume their wonted position as citizens of the United States, *not* in a spirit of hostility, but with the patriotic desire to honor the Government protecting them.

In the next half century a new generation rebuilt the county and brought it to new plateaus of accomplishment. The war proved one thing for certain—that these were people of vitality and courage who were willing to give whatever effort necessary for a place that had become much more than a temporary jumping off point for the next ridge to be climbed, the next river to be crossed, or the next frontier to be tamed. This vitality would be translated into new levels of progress in every aspect of community development, and the foundations for the twentieth century would be laid.

Industrial and Community Growth

In 1951 Sir Eric Bowater of the English paper-making empire was concerned with expanding his worldwide operation to the United States. Calhoun was selected as the site of Bowaters' new American plant. The reasons that Calhoun was chosen in 1951 were precisely the same reasons that it was important to the Indians and first white settlers: excellent natural resources, centrality to transportation, and, most particularly, the abundantly available waters of the Hiwassee. Today, the Calhoun Bowaters plant is the largest producer of newsprint in the world, and one of a long list of mills in East Tennessee.

The first mills to appear in the county ground corn and wheat. Later, the first cotton spinning mill in East Tennessee was erected on Mouse Creek in the 1830s by Ephraim Slack. An old newspaper report from that time states that the mill could do the work of 100 women laboring at spinning wheels. Ephraim Slack drowned in the mill pond a few years later and one of his sons, John, went on to become a leading newspaperman in the state.

From about 1850 until the 1890's, when it was destroyed by fire, a spinning mill in the Mt. Verd area was one of the biggest industrial operations in the county. It was located to the left of the double bridges at Mt. Verd and was owned originally by Charles W. Metcalf. It came to be known as the McElwee Mill when that family took over its operation.

This was the beginning of a textile industry which has continued to thrive in the county with companies such as Chilhowee, Van Raalte, Crescent Hosiery, Athens Hosiery, and Beaunit each having its period of importance. Finally, in the late 1930s, the same resource that powered the mills was used by the Tennessee Valley Authority to produce electrical power with water-driven turbines. The industrial development of the county has always been closely associated with its multitude of water resources.

One early mill was operated by the Saulpaw family one mile east of Calhoun at the spot where the Eastanallee Creek runs into the Hiwassee River. While the mill itself was torn down following the TVA acquisitions in the area, the old dam still remains. The Saulpaws produced a popular brand of flour known as "Silver Queen." In the 1921 centennial edition of a now extinct publication called *The Semi-Weekly Post*, G. L. Saulpaw remarked that business was good, but that he had been at the work so long that "he would sell if a suitable buyer presented himself." The imposing Saulpaw grave marker in the old cemetery next to the Calhoun Baptist Church is one of the most elaborate in the county.

An even more notable success was the Long family's opera-

The Long family's Athens Roller Mills

tion of the Athens Roller Mill which continued on the Eastanallee near the heart of the Athens business district until the most recent times. "Morning Glory Flour" and "Long's Perfection Self-Rising Flour" were as popular in their day as Mayfield's milk is today. The Long milling operation later extended to other parts of the county.

Mills quickly diversified with flume lines typically driving at least two turbines in the same mill. The Riley Thompson mill near Riceville was five stories high, and, in addition to the grist operation, housed the furniture shop of Hamilton Jarnigan. The machinery in Elisha Dotson's mill turned a saw for cutting timber, powered wool and cotton carding equipment, and did the traditional corn and wheat grinding. A precursor of the "mill town" appeared near the Frank Gettys mill in the lower Eastanallee valley, where a special type of cotton material called "ducking" was produced. Elliot Keith produced rag paper stock at

Glenmore which was one of the first six paper mills operating in the state.

The water-powered mills ultimately gave way to advanced technology. By 1901, for example, J. W. Trew operated a steam-powered cotton gin at Dentville east of Calhoun near the Polk County line. As late as 1968, thirteen bales of cotton were ginned here. The old Trew store continues today as a relic of a bygone era. One can move from one era to another by leaving the Bowaters mill at Calhoun and driving 13 miles across to Highway 411, through the Trew family settlement, and then to the old mill town of Pendergast, now called Delano.

The era of the water-powered mill may be gone, but memories of the beauty, the sounds, and the visible power of the old gears and turbines persist in the minds of the remaining few who experienced their operation. The humming whine and staccato clicking of the modern computerized factory pale by comparison.

Nothing quite captures the old mill experience like J. A. Butterfield's famous ballad "When You and I Were Young, Maggie." This is one of the best-known songs of the entire "country" music heritage, and interestingly enough had its antecedents in McMinn County. George Johnson was born on the Hiwassee and, while going to look for gold in the Unakas, came upon a mill along the present L&N line between Etowah and Reliance. There he met and later married Marrie Harris—"Maggie." After living on the Hiwassee for many years, they returned to visit the old mill. Here, in a moment of inspired reflection, Johnson wrote the poem that later became the basis for Butterfield's famous song.

The industrial expansion and accompanying population growth that reached beyond the time of the great water mills would have been severely handicapped had it not been for the appearance of railroads in the county. In fact, railroad construction, from the development of the first important communities in the county outside of Athens and Calhoun, to the creation of the major railroading and community center at Etowah in 1906, to the building of the 9.2 mile L&N spur to Bowaters in 1961 which was the longest new track construction by L&N since the 1940s, has always been at the center of expansion in the county. It should also be made clear that the railroad did not simply come to McMinn County by accident. It was because of the support of the general population of McMinn County that the first railroad construction project in Tennessee occurred here.

The railroads were to an earlier time what interstate highways have been to the present time. This is no small consideration, especially when one compares the industrialization and growth of McMinn County to its neighboring county of Meigs which is still the only county in the state which has no rail line at all. Consider also the way that growth in McMinn County lagged behind that of Bradley County in recent years because of the longer time that it took for the interstate system to be completed in McMinn. In every respect, the decisions which brought the railroads into McMinn were of highest significance and the result of enlightened and progressive minds.

The story of the Hiwassee Rail Road, which became the East Tennessee, Virginia, and Georgia Railroad and ultimately a part of the Southern Railroad system in 1894, is told in detail by James Burn in *The Daily Post-Athenian Sesqui-centennial Edition.*

One of the persons primarily responsible for bringing the first railroad through McMinn County was James Hayes Reagan, who was elected to the state senate in 1835. He was assisted in the legislature by John Miller, representing McMinn County, and Elijah Hurst, representing both McMinn and Monroe counties. These men were later joined by R. C. Jackson, for whom Jackson Street in Athens is named (not Andrew Jackson as most assume). Jackson even went so far as to bring in Samuel P. Ivins, the county's first prominent newspaper man, to establish the *Athens Post* for the primary reason of convincing the general populace, who would ultimately have to help with financing, on the idea of railroads.

In addition to the accomplishments of these men and others who will be named, two other factors made the route through McMinn attractive. First, the area was not mountainous, and secondly, there had already existed for some time a major stage route that ran from Dalton, Georgia, to Cleveland and then to

J. H. Reagan, the guiding spirit behind the early railroad development

Athens. It then went to Greenback where there was a ferry crossing the Tennessee River, and beyond the river into Knoxville. Those who originated the railroad idea decided to follow this route from Dalton to Athens, but then head directly up the Sweetwater Valley (where Reagan had large land holdings) to Blair's Ferry (present-day Loudon), where goods and passengers could be ferried and carried on into Knoxville.

In 1836 the Tennessee legislature approved a proposal by which the state would provide one-third capital funding, if two-thirds could be raised by subscription, to finance a railroad project. The Hiwassee Rail Road Company was immediately formed. The initial plan was to sell 4000 shares at $100.00 per share by January 1, 1837.

By this time, however, only $120,000 had been raised, so six McMinn Countians—Asbury Coffey, James Fyffe, Alexander Keyes, Onslow Murrell, Nathaniel Smith, and T. Nixon Van Dyke—personally secured the balance. The stockholders held their first meeting in Athens and elected Solomon Jacobs of Knoxville president. They ordered surveys conducted, rights-of-way secured, and a two-story headquarters building constructed by the Cleages in Athens. The structure, referred to as the "Cleage Building" earlier, still stands next to the Federal Building on North Jackson Street.

The stockholders first anticipated that the 98¼ mile project—figured at a cost of $11,500 per mile, including bridges over the Hiwassee at Calhoun and the Tennessee at Loudon—would cost $1,250,000. By mid-1839 work was halted. Almost $936,329 had been spent, and all there was to show for it was a bridge at Calhoun, 66 miles of graded roadbed, and a partially completed iron manufacturing plant at Charleston which had been haphazardly conceived as a major money-saving enterprise to supply the builders with their own spikes and rails.

Because of a variety of legal and legislature actions, charter revisions, and new attempts at financing, work was not resumed until 1849. As a part of these revisions, the corporation became the East Tennessee and Georgia Railroad. Representative David Ballew and Senator William Cooke of McMinn County had worked diligently to bring the new charter into existence. Alexander Keyes was elected president, with T. Nixon Van Dyke, W. F. Keith, and R. C. Morris among the directors. Officials held ground-breaking ceremonies in Dalton in June of 1849 at the southern terminal.

Work now proceeded quickly and without many problems. In fact, as each new mile of track stretched northward huge public fanfare, free barbeques, and inspired oratory were held—all designed to increase the already burgeoning public support. By February of 1852 tracks had reached Mouse Creek (present-day Niota), Sweetwater by April, and finally by July the river at Loudon. In 1854, on property bought from the heirs of James

Willson, Sr., the ET&Ga built a depot at Mouse Creek, the oldest still in use in Tennessee.

The northbound passenger train left Dalton at 2:30 P.M.; it was due at Varnell's at 2:57, at Red Clay at 3:15, at Blue Spring at 3:42, at Cleveland at 3:54, at Charleston at 4:30, at Riceville at 4:51, at Athens at 5:15, at Mouse Creek at 5:35, at Sweetwater at 5:57, and at Philadelphia at 6:15. It was scheduled to arrive at Loudon at 6:35 P.M. The southbound train left Loudon at 4:00 A.M. and arrived at Dalton at 8:30 A.M. An additional freight train ran from each terminal daily with a maximum of 20 cars loaded to 16,000 pounds (according to Burn, the amount carried by three freight cars today).

In mid-1852 James Gettys of Athens received the contract to build the Loudon bridge. He employed George W. Saulpaw, a stone mason from the North, to build the piers; the superstructure was subcontracted. By the middle of 1855 it was possible to go from Dalton to Knoxville by rail. The ET&G planned a grand "Railroad Jubilee and Fourth of July Celebration" and offered the celebrants a special $4.00 round-trip fare from Knoxville to Dalton. Although in 1851 Athens was designated the main center of operations, in 1856 under the direction of new president Campbell Wallace, the headquarters were moved to Knoxville. One can only speculate what McMinn County would be like today if it had become a major southeastern railway center.

The role of the ET&Ga in the Civil War has already been mentioned. Senator Reagan, one of its founders, had been a Union supporter, but gave his final allegiance to his southern homeland. He was kidnapped late in the war by the Union army and held ransom for a northern prisoner being held in the South named Joseph Monroe. Efforts on both the northern and southern sides to secure his release were too slow, and Reagan died from the overexposure to the elements he experienced during confinement.

Later generations of McMinn Countians watched huge steam engines and sleek diesels cover the lines surveyed and built by these pioneer entrepreneurs. The station at Athens finally met the same fate as passenger service, and its absence continues to be mourned by those who used it as a point of reference for the entire community. Today, part of the old station has been incorporated into the structures of the Tennessee Valley Railroad Museum in Chattanooga.

Names like those of agents J. W. Fisher and Fred Snyder, engineers Charles Brackett, Buster Dunn, C. H. Henritze, and especially their trains—"The Tennessean," "The Birmingham Special," and "The Pelican," which became famous in the first half of the twentieth century—still remain to recall a rich moment in the county's heritage.

During the 1890s the Knoxville Southern Railroad built a line that cut across the eastern side of the county and connected Knoxville to Atlanta by a new route, thus opening an almost entirely untouched section to the kind of commercial success that the ET&Ga had brought to the Sweetwater Valley. This second road soon merged with the Marietta and North Georgia Railroad to become the Atlanta, Knoxville, and Northern Railroad. It ran from Knoxville through Monroe County to Tellico Junction (Englewood), and ten miles south of the junction took an abrupt cut toward the spectacular Hiwassee River Gorge and then on to Marietta.

In 1904 construction of a new line from this cut-off point south of Tellico Junction straight through to Cartersville was begun. The town of Etowah was established at this time and soon became the repair center and headquarters of the Atlanta division of what was by then a part of the Louisville and Nashville Railroad. By 1925 more than 2000 persons were employed at the Etowah operation and 21 trains (14 passenger and 7 freight) came through the Etowah station. The old station, which had been allowed to deteriorate, has recently been restored into a beautiful landmark.

With the exception of renewed activity caused by World War II, the Etowah operation began to decline in the 1930s. The shops were oriented to repair wooden cars which became obsolete, and company headquarters were consolidated at Knoxville. Today, Etowah railroading activities primarily involve shipments from Copperhill and the large pulpwood and paper traffic associated with Bowaters. Many people in Etowah with close ties to the L&N still remember famous passenger trains of the early and mid twentieth century such as "The Southland," "The Georgian," and "The Flamingo."

Finally, in 1887, the Tellico Railroad Company was incorporated to build a 22-mile line from Athens to Tellico Plains. This opened a relatively unexploited timber and mining area to rail service in a more profitable manner. The road was in operation a little over a year later.

An important community grew up in 1870 two miles southeast of the place where the new Tellico line crossed the AK&N line at a place which became known as Tellico Junction. Jacob, James, and Mortimer Brient, who had already become noteworthy for establishing the Hickory Flat Roller Mills and the Jersey Herd and Dairy east of Athens, built several shops, mills, and houses to take advantage of the railroad construction. By 1907 the locus of commerce had so completely shifted to Tellico Junction that the Eureka Cotton Mill moved there, becoming the primary establishment in town. The following year the community's name was changed to Englewood at the suggestion of Miss Nannie Chesnutt, sister of James Brient's wife, because it reminded her of the wooded home of Robin Hood she had read about as a child. In 1901 the Brients had joined J. W. Chesnutt in building a flour and feed mill called the Englewood Milling Company, and in 1917 Chesnutt joined with a Knoxville group to establish a hosiery mill, the Englewood Manufacturing Company.

The terms "Yellow Top," "Socktown," and "Onion Hill" still are important designations that came to describe the tenement communities of the Eureka, Englewood Manufacturing, and Englewood Milling companies respectively. As at Etowah, the Great Depression of the 1930s took a severe toll on Englewood industry.

An uncredited article, "Gem of the Unakas," reveals a unique aspect of life in Englewood in the early 1920s:

> If we envied anybody, it would be the quiet, happy people of the splendid little city of Englewood. Her women, as well as the men, are wide awake business people. The women are playing an important role in its development: a woman is the president of the

White Cliffs Springs resort hotel

Eureka Hosiery; a woman, Miss Sallie Smith, is assistant cashier of the Bank of Englewood and is also a member of the Board of Directors; a woman, Mrs. Heath, runs the principal hotel; a woman, Mrs. Tallent, runs a first class boarding house; and women, Mrs. Chesnutt and her daughters, Misses Grace and Nannie, run a 600 acre farm.

The Tellico Railroad line itself prospered until 1911 when it was taken over by the L&N, which allowed this line to extend its operations to Athens. The train left Athens each morning at ten, made eight stops before reaching Tellico Plains, and then returned to Athens by shortly after four in the afternoon. In 1983 the line from Englewood to Tellico Plains was abandoned.

The most interesting stop may have been at White Cliff station where passengers made connections with carriages to the White Cliff Springs Resort on Starr's Mountain. Once a summer residence for the very wealthy similar to Lookout Mountain in

Chattanooga, by the early 1900s an exquisite resort had been established. The mineral water springs and clear mountain air made it one of the most popular resorts in the nation. The first pike road—Mecca Pike—built in the county connected Athens with these springs. In 1914 the hotel went out of business and for a few years the resort operated as the White Cliff Club in which accommodations were owned by different individuals, much like today's condominiums. Several wealthy families from the county participated in this venture.

Two conductors on the Tellico line gained a high reputation. M. M. Miller left the railroad to establish Miller Brothers Department Store in Etowah. J. W. Gregory worked for fifty years and retired in the late 1950s when passenger service on the line was eliminated. Another well-known personality was Etowah's Sid Garwood who served the L&N line as an engineer for many years. Garwood brought the first train into Etowah on December 6, 1906. Garwood's two brothers were also famous L&N railroaders.

The late 1800s and early 1900s were a time of vigorous industrial growth throughout the United States, and no better example could be found than McMinn County. There were numerous spinoffs of the railroads. For example, A. E. Walthall and F. O. Mahery established a crosstie yard that at one time was shipping one and a half million board feet of lumber per month to major railroads throughout the northern and eastern part of the country.

Improved communications and transportation became signs of the time, and McMinn Countians took advantage of them. As early as 1888, Mr. and Mrs. T. J. Long established a crude telephone system by stringing a long wire from their business across the street to their home; they used tin cups on each end as transmitters and receivers. In 1912 another progressive citizen contributed to the decline of the livery business by introducing the first taxi, and by the 1920s the Tennessee Coach Company had brought bus service to the county. But it was the railroads that rushed the county into the modern age.

One of the most ambitious projects ever to begin in McMinn County involved the establishment, in 1887, of the Athens Mining and Manufacturing Company. The grand scheme of the new company included a model industrial and residential community on 800 acres in the North Athens section of the city using the present Woodward Avenue as the main street. This involved street and utility construction and space for churches and recreation. Funds for the model city were to include at least the following: $100,000 to start a woolen mill; $100,000 to construct a cotton plaid mill; $90,000 for a cotton sheeting mill; $60,000 for a cotton warp mill; $60,000 for a warp mill exclusively to produce jeans; $30,000 for a majestic hotel; $10,000 for a new public school; whatever was necessary for a new water system; and cooperation in the venture of a railroad to Tellico Plains.

The original charter was signed by R. L. Bright, R. J. Fisher, F. W. McElwee, W. M. Nixon, George W. Ochs, A. C. Robeson, and John L. Young, Jr. Bright served as the first president, Fisher was the first general manager, and W. Gettys became the first vice president. The company was ambitiously constituted, to quote from its charter, for the following purposes:

> carrying on the business of mining for coal, copper, zinc, mica, iron, or other ore or mineral including the operation of quarrying for slate, limestone, or marble, and for sinking shafts or boring for petroleum, rock oil, salt water, or other valuable liquids hidden in the earth, and for the business of manufacturing any raw material by the aid of machinery into articles suitable for use as cotton and woolen factories, for making bagging and bale rope or iron bands for baling cotton, forming implements or other articles whether from iron or wood, and in general of carrying on of any other business properly coming within the definition of a manufactory.

The company conducted an aggressive advertising campaign throughout the eastern United States. Prospective investors received special railroad rates to come and see the property, and eventually people in Ohio, Pennsylvania, Wisconsin, Georgia, and Tennessee bought stock. In June of 1887, when the first lots were sold, $500,000 was supposed to be spent on the site within three years. The whole concept was an excellent example of American utopianism at its best.

Unfortunately, for a combination of reasons, by 1889 the cor-

R. J. Fisher, entrepreneur and inventor who brought the county national attention

poration was in desperate financial circumstances, involved in a number of lawsuits, and faced foreclosure. Perhaps the most compelling problem was that many other communities across the nation were involved in similar projects and promised payments by investors often did not materialize. In addition, Knoxville and Chattanooga were more rapidly growing markets which lured good businesses away and were more attractive to prospective firms looking for new locations. An excellent example is the foundry and machine shop of George Wheland which was established in Athens in 1868, but which moved to Chattanooga and continues to be a principal business of that city as one of the main suppliers of the auto industry in the Southeast. (The Wheland name descended from the ancient Anglo-Saxon mythological hero "Wayland the Smith" who was conceived to be the semidivine forerunner of iron workers.)

R. J. Fisher, who established the first hosiery mill in Athens, brought the first bicycle to town, and became the first McMinn Countian to ride in an airplane, gained patents on a new typewriter concept that led to the establishment of the Fisher Typewriter Factory; however, since the business centers of the country were in the Northeast, the company moved first to Cleveland, Ohio, and then to Harrisburg, Pennsylvania.

In spite of the fact that the grand scheme failed, the area did become significantly industrialized, and factories and mills continued to be an important aspect of the economy in this area into the modern age. Owners of the Athens Hosiery Mill quickly completed their part of the project and also built a considerable number of tenement dwellings; this mill remains. A furniture manufactory also started operations, and its traditions are continued today by other companies in the same area of town such as Athens Bed Company, Athens Table Company, Carver Manufacturing Company, and McKeehan Chair. The water works planned in the original scheme became operational, making "Water Tank Hill" a focal point of the community. To keep pace with development in the area, city fathers were busy with street construction.

The crowning glory of the whole project was the mining corporation's hotel. The building, called "The Grand View Hotel," was a magnificent architectural achievement and along with the R. J. Fisher residence, on the present site of the First Baptist Church, represented the most advanced and aesthetically pleasing design of the day. The hotel, which was never actually completed by the corporation, was ultimately sold to Grant University (the precursor of Tennessee Wesleyan College) in 1892 and was known as Parker College. The building was struck by lightning

The R. J. Fisher home on the site of the present First Baptist Church

on July 10, 1907, and burned in one of the most famous fires of the county's history. Either sarcastically or affectionately the building came to be known as the "Red Elephant." After it burned, John and Gus Kelley cleaned the bricks for 10¢ per 100, and their father Joseph hauled them to the Tennessee Wesleyan campus. There they were used as an interior wall in a new construction project.

In his short memoir Charles F. Keith, Jr., detailed what the

The Grand View Hotel, known as the "Red Elephant"

city square of Athens looked like in 1870. Corners were typically given names related to long-term ownership or because of residences that had at one time existed on the particular sites. Although these names may be confusing to the outsider, natives continue to use them to describe locations.

A hardware store owned by T. F. Gibson stood on the southeast corner of the square at the intersection of White Street and Madison Avenue. In later years, the busy Newton's Bus Station and Restaurant seved as a hub for travelers coming into the county. Across the street to the north, where for many years there was an A&P grocery store and in more recent years a variety of discount stores stood the residence and dry goods store of W. G. Horton. Beyond that on the longtime site of Cherokee Hadware Company was the three-story Bayless hardware store—this corner was called the "Dewitt Corner."

Continuing north and crossing Jackson Street the "Ballew Corner" was once occupied by a laundry and tailor shop run by two men named Levi and Chang; by 1870 the Hortons had a drugstore there which continued under family ownership until recent times. This corner is now a parking lot.

West across Madison Avenue, where the Robert E. Lee Hotel stands today, was the "Henderson Corner"; before the hotel was built, it had been a stagecoach headquarters. The present hotel was built in 1926 by G. J. Lockmiller using some of the finest marbles available. "Slim" Armstrong was a thirteen-year-old bellhop and across the years became as much of an institution as the hotel itself. "Lizzie" Fisher had once had a hat shop on this site.

Continuing along this side of the street, the next corner was identified with the McKeldin family. Will and John Horton had a dry goods store here, and in later years—before the shopping center era—Proffit's Department Store was highly successful.

Across Washington Street on the site long occupied by the First National Bank was the "McGaughey Corner." There was a large tin shop here which reached back toward the present Tuell's Grocery, which has become something of a local landmark in recent years. The Forees came in later years and established their first medical practice on this block before moving, in 1930, to the city's first hospital, which they had built.

Moving south across Jackson Street to the corner recently occupied by Woolworth's, and once occupied by Riddle's Drugs before it moved down the block and became Riddle and Wallace, was the location of Dutch Cunningham's Drugs. Above the drugstore was an exclusive private association, the Eastanalle Club, where the self-appointed business and professional elite of the community regularly convened. Many of the important political, social, and economic decisions affecting the community were made within the confines of this circle.

Moving along to the site occupied by the Strand Theatre and Heird's Drugs was the "Atlee Corner," and across White Street at the old First Farmers Bank location was the "Grubb Corner." A large, open ditch, with several bridges and crosswalks, ran along the west side of White Street from Depot Hill to the Eastanallee Creek (the Indian spelling, Oostanaula, is often used today) and for many years was a source of great consternation to the citizenry.

Mule trading day in Athens before the turn of the century

Finally, to the east across Washington Street on the "Crow Corner" was a meat and produce market run by Jim Crow and a grocery store run by his son, George. On down the block to the present Citizens Bank, where Miller's Department Store with its unique cable-and-cup money-carrying system once stood, was the "Crawford Corner." Yet another dry goods store and a public well originally occupied this location.

Tradition says, according to Keith, that the McGaughey Corner was the gathering place of those of Whig/Unionist sentiments, and the Crawford Corner the focal point of old Democrat/Confederate persuasion. On many occasions the air around the square was highly charged with political tension. It was not unusual for tempers to become aroused and for blows to be struck. In a later generation, this same square erupted in a political explosion which would be heard throughout the nation.

Before the turn of the century a narrow gauge track ran from Depot Hill down present-day Jackson Street, turned left at the square, and ran on out toward where the First Baptist Church is today. The track stopped at what was then Tobe Getty's cornfield. George Brown operated the small car, which was pulled by a team of mules.

Weston A. Goodspeed's biographical sketches in *History of East Tennessee* provide only brief glimpses, but leave little doubt that there were vigorous, intelligent, industrious, and ambitious people in the county after the Civil War. William Dixon came to McMinn County with 25¢ and a suit of clothes; by 1886 he was worth $10,000. George W. Foster, who "made himself quite famous as a horse dealer," was a Republican and served with the Federal forces "during the late war." "He is not a member of any church, but believes in the Bible. His wife is a professor of religion, but had not yet connected herself with any church." William L. Harbison, after serving with the Confederate forces, returned to East Tennessee in 1869; "but as someone attempted to assassinate him, for safety he resided in Decatur and other points in Tennessee....He returned to Athens in 1875 where he had a lucrative law practice....The Harbisons are of Irish extraction and, without exception, Democrats." James M. Henderson, president of the First National Bank, represented the county at the constitutional convention in Nashville in 1865. James Howard Hood, who founded the *McMinn Citizen* newspaper, "advanced so rapidly in his studies that he passed examinations and became a public school teacher at the age of seventeen." About 1885 he left his teaching position to become the railroad station agent at Mouse Creek (Niota). James T. Johnson was wounded in the hand at Fort Donelson, "and was saved from another by his cartridge box, which stopped a bullet." He was captured and imprisoned for seven months at Camp Morton in Indianapolis. By 1886 he was a "well-to-do farmer." J. H. Lusk "located in Athens in 1879...and is one of the most popular and efficient salesmen in the county, where he is universally known and highly respected." The merchant Benjamin F. Martin was a self-made and highly respected man, who came to Calhoun with only a wife and a pony. Frank B. McElwee, who manufactured cotton goods, "belonged to the U.S. Army Secret Service and...at different times piloted the Union Army through the mountains of East Tennessee." James Oliphant, who was retired at the time Goodspeed wrote, began his medical practice with only $5, and by the beginning of the war was worth over $15,000. Joseph C. Rucker, well-known and enterprising farmer, "went to Nashville to join the Union Army, but decided to return home and protect his mother." James P. Thompson, after one year of study under Dr. T. J. Evans in Charleston, was ready to practice dentistry, which he did for nine years. He was also a successful trader in livestock, mules and horses. James D. Williams, leading merchant and postmaster at Williamsburg, "began life a poor man, but by industry and careful management has accumulated a fair portion of the world's goods." He was a Royal Arch Mason, a Democrat, and a straight prohibitionist. William P. Willson, well-known and enterprising planter who owned nearly 520 acres, "has been a live and progressive man, but not ambitious for wealth." These detailed here, and others like them, gave to McMinn County the sweat of their brow and the strength of their hearts.

A large number of individuals and businesses became firmly established in the county during the period immediately following World War I. The growing economy allowed for the creation of a professional and business establishment that served as the cornerstone for community growth over the next half century. A brief description of the leading businesses and professions, based on the 1921 centennial edition of *The Semi-Weekly Post*, is in order.

Live Oaks Farms was the predecessor of the regionally well-known Mayfield Dairy Farms. A 1922 advertisement read: "T. B. Mayfield and Son are among the best farmers of the county....Cattle Tuberculine Tested—dairy products from tuberculine tested cattle should command your first consideration, and its importance cannot be overestimated." The Mayfield operation also included the sale of cattle, horses, mules, and "famous" Berkshire hogs.

In 1928 F. O. Mahery, Sr., who had been involved in the Walthall and Mahery lumber and crosstie operation, took over leadership of the Athens Stove Works which had opened in

Mayfield's Dairy Farms—perhaps the best known business in the county

1924. In the 33 years of Mahery's presidency, the company moved from wood and coal stoves to gas in 1932 and electric in 1956. The company motto, "Vesta Stoves for Better Living —Everywhere," became a national slogan.

After it introduced a new tractor plow invented by Jay Stevenson, who worked for McMinn Motor Company, the Athens Plow Company became a major industrial concern in the county. E. L. Willson, its president, established himself as a key leader in the local business community. In the mid-1940s J. H. Taylor moved from Athens Plow to produce his own farm equipment inventions at Taylor Implement Manufacturing Company. The Dennis Foundry did much of the casting of heavy metal for the local industries.

The Athens Furniture Company, which became Athens Table and Manufacturing Company, was owned by the Hoback family. Carl, Richard, and Sarah Bayless were instrumental in the company's operation. The *Post* chronicler said of Sarah that "her untiring interest has proven how valuable the services of a woman may become."

The success of the Athens Hosiery Mill resulted from the creativity and genius of R. J. Fisher, Sr. His sons: R. J., Jr., who had strong design and technical expertise, and Ed, whose camaraderie with the mill employees is still well-remembered in

North Athens, later managed the firm. The mill became famous for its "Spartan," "Takoma Pear," and "Maid of Athens" brands which were distributed throughout the world. The products of this mill were probably the first to represent McMinn County internationally.

There were three drugstores in 1921. The Horton family had been important to the business development of the county almost since its inception, and Joe Horton had operated Horton and Sons Drugs, with his son Glen, for 48 years. The *Post* writer was correct in saying that Miles A. Riddle in eleven years had built "a business which will remain one of Athens' greater institutions during the years to come." Ed Heird, who was from Meigs County, worked for Riddle and later opened his own drugstore on the same block. Of the Julian Pharmacy, which no longer exists, the *Post* rhapsodized: "his soda jerker juggles a wicked glass. His fountain dispenses all the frozen and semi-artistic dainties usually found in a metropolitan palace of sweets, which causes the cash register to tinkle merrily."

There were a large variety of general merchandise and hardware stores which by the early 1920s had begun to develop specialties. The J. W. Colston Store had been in operation since 1894. The J. Nat Moore Hardware was the leading name in feed and seed sales in the county for many years. Today, it specializes in home appliances. Bayless Hardware had just added a furniture and music department, and Lackey Hardware, with Leuty Owen as its main clerk, had begun to sell Buick automobiles. Lackey's full-page Christmas ad offered the chance to win a 75-piece dinnerware set worth $65.00, a considerable amount for that time.

Ford vehicles were sold by McMinn Motor Company which continues to exist. The dealership was led by Cyril Jones, brother of the important political figure Clem Jones, and Hugh Lowery. Marshall J. Keith sold Chevrolets and Studebakers at Athens Motor Company. Gasoline for these automobiles was provided by Dixie Filling Station where, according to the *Post*, W. E. Clark "exchanges the product of John D. for the product of the United States Mint." The big selling feature was "visible gas" and the company carried Mansfield, Silvertown, Oxford, and Remington tires. R. J. Haley Rubber Company sold tires and vulcanized its own rubber.

Insurance companies were popular during this period. Dodson Insurance Agency, the oldest in the county, was founded by William Calvin Dodson in 1899 and operated until 1968 under the able and memorable direction of Frank Dodson. It was recently merged into the Athens Insurance Agency. L. H. Hoback, one of the best-known music directors in the region, and C. F. Keith, Jr., the ranking major of the state national guard, also headed insurance agencies.

J. H. Neil, father of the well-known Joe Wheeler Neil, operated a grocery store at the corner of Jackson and Washington Street for many years. D. B. Shoemaker and his wife Marie, a war bride from France, opened a grocery business which was so successful the store building itself fell in because of the weight of the stock that had to be kept on hand. Bud Steed operated the first "chain" grocery with two locations in the county. In the 1960s, in spite of the entrance of national grocery chains into the community, Alfred McKeehan started a local store which eventually had branches in most of the counties of southeast Tennessee.

In addition to the clothes that were sold in the general merchandise stores, specialty apparel shops were established. Owen and Company was highly visible for many years on the square in Athens. James Cravey, a salesperson, later opened his own dry goods store. Kate Fox operated a hat shop (a millinery), and the Smith Bootery claimed to be able to "fit the pedal extremities of either Cinderella or Goliath." In 1915 Morris Goodfriend became the first important Jewish merchant in the county. The Goodfriend name continues to be identified with the finest in men's wear. In later years Simon Monen continued the tradition of excellent Jewish business establishments in the community.

The First National Bank, established in 1872, came to prominence with leaders such as J. M. Henderson, James Hornsby, R. M., R. J., and James G. Fisher, Clem Jones, and S. F. Gettys. The former downtown branch building had just been completed in 1921 and was the showplace of East Tennessee according to the local promotions. In 1938 Pat Love came to Athens from

Morristown and bought controlling interest in the First Farmers Bank from Tom Sherman. On May 1, 1940, he assumed presidency of the bank and, along with his brother Founta, operated the well-known institution until 1968. The bank was eventually sold to a group of businessmen from Memphis who were backed by the First National Bank of that city.

Finally, there were several highly specialized businesses which were doing well during the postwar period. The Strand Theatre, which was called "The Palace" until 1916 and was the first movie house in the county to succeed, continued in operation until about 1980. W. W. Padgett Marble Company sent exquisite Tennessee and Georgia marble throughout the world. Coming from a far corner of the world for that day, Dr. J. A. Saliba of Betargin, Syria, opened a sanitorium on the site of the present Hammer-Johnson Supply Company. The hospital was in the Blizzard House, a mansionlike building across the street from the Monday House, another local hotel.

Of the varied material in *The Semi-Weekly Post* special edition, the description of the Athens Steam Laundry is the most unforgettable. Under the heading "Let Her Live a Little Longer" and the subheading "Olliker Walliker, Olliker Rocks, Let the Laundry Wash Your Socks," the business of the youthful, enterprising Cecil Martin is thus saluted:

> When the average resident of Athens learns that the wife's energy, effort and muscle is worth considerable more than the dime necessary to "get the laundry to do it," and that sanitation as a general thing is a minus quality in the laundry of "Aunt Diana," and that the Athens Steam Laundry employs no chink to squirt and spray the water through his nose over the delicate kerchief and the buttonless night shirt, then and then only will the business of the Athens Steam Laundry pick up, materially.

In 1921 the object of the greatest excitement in the county was the work on the state's first concrete highway which was being constructed from the Hiwassee River north to Athens. The paving of streets in Athens to join with this modern Lee Highway became a source of great civic pride.

The first highly mechanized equipment used to work county roads. In this 1923 photograph the caterpillar is pulling a road grader.

The rock for the highway project was dug and crushed at the present site of Knox Park. A short section of the road still exists from the city of Calhoun to U.S. Highway 11. As a young man in his early twenties, my father, Bob Byrum, was employed by the state to test the concrete. This involved drilling out a core every fifty feet, with each new hole one foot over from the preceding one. It was undoubtedly a laborious process to follow this pattern the 14 miles from the Hiwassee River bridge to the Athens city limits. The road-builders were making history, and there was always a curious and inquisitive group of onlookers to help pass the day.

In 1933 J. M. Sharp published a personal memoir entitled *Recollections and Hearsays of Athens Fifty Years and Beyond* which constitutes the most detailed historical recollection of McMinn County, and particularly Athens, to date. Sharp had been involved in a variety of occupations that included teaching school and delivering newspapers. He had a distinct flair for words and, in addition to his historical material, had published poetry and a booklet entitled "Letters to the Man in the Moon." Sharp's record provides at least a glimpse at important figures between the wars.

During this particular period the community probably had as many physicians as at any time in its history. Dr. J. R. Nankiville was the oldest doctor in town and, in addition to his medical work, contributed immeasurably to the advancement of education in the area. Dr. J. L. Proudfoot (who had practiced from a house on the Eastanallee between the present Cooke Box and Mayfield's) had just died and the community had given his family a house so that they could remain in Athens. Dr. J. O. Foree, who had established a clinic, had passed from the scene but his two sons, Ed and Carey, were carrying on in the hospital they established in 1930. Dr. L. W. Spradling was well-known for his avocations; he was a mechanic, writer, and landscape painter, and according to Sharp "an all around versatile genius, a radiator of sunshine." Drs. Ross Arrants, Brock, Dubois, Roy Epperson (who opened a second hospital in January of 1936), and Janeway completed the list of physicians. In addition to these men, Dr. G. W. Stanton had become popular as the physician identified with North Athens.

The primary building material of the period was wood, so lumber yards and building supply houses were important. Tom Sherman, who may be the richest man in the county's history, and Mel Hammer owned the Sherman-Hammer Company. Hugh and Charles Hoback operated the Athens Planing Mill; the Duckworth Planing Mill was also prominent. Furniture was another necessity so the Johnson and McSpadden families entered the county business community in the time between the wars; both continue to be prominent. Among the attorneys represented were Judge S. C. Brown and E. B. Madison who had been in the area for the longest period of time in 1933. H. M. Chandler, in addition to his legal activities in the county, had served 24 years in the state legislature; Jimmie Clark and Tom Taylor had each been in the legislature for one term. Clem Jones and R. A. Davis became prominent because of their involvement with both the Southern and L&N railroads. Among the younger men in the profession were Paul Stewart and R. N. Ivins.

Among the teachers mentioned by Sharp were Professor J. C. Ridenour, who had been principal at Forrest Hill School for eighteen years, and Professor J. H. Walker, who had been principal of North Athens School. Mrs. Laura Sliger and Annie Sliger taught for many years in the city school system.

A DeSoto-Plymouth Agency opened under the management of Mitchell Hanks and J. M. Millard; Mooney Tallent and Dillard Brown worked here. Another garage was operated by the Wilkins family. Mrs. R. J. McKeldin was the local florist and there were two undertakers, that owned by Harry Evans and the new Quissenberry and Forrest. Sharp concluded his list of luminaries by remembering his own colleagues, the paper carriers, about whom he said: "We carry papers to the palace of the rich and the hovel of the poor, and thus we help the knights of the quill."

Industrial and community growth in the county was not confined to Athens. Tobe Gettys, who owned a woolen mill south of Riceville, constructed a depot on the Southern line and named it "Sanford" after a prominent Knoxville family. This small community was also the home of a large business in the production and shipment or railroad ties. Meanwhile, by the early part of the twentieth century, the names of Bolen, Henry, and McAlister had become important in Calhoun business circles. Dr. H. F. Taylor, who served a good deal of the county from his office in Calhoun, cannot be omitted.

The names of Bishop, Erickson, Oliphant, Parkinson, Porter, Swafford, and Womac came to be of lasting important in Riceville. The remains of the old Porter house (recently gutted by fire) still stand south of Riceville on U.S. Highway 11. Charlie Miller restored the house and used the land to develop one of the largest pedigreed Angus cattle farms in the state.

Charles Rice, founder of the town, organized a train of 50 wagons and moved to Arkansas in 1859. C. W. Oliphant clerked in the store that Rice sold to a relative, and later established his own mercantile business before selling out to J. M. Lockmiller and becoming a famed salesman. Dan Roberts became an important business figure after expanding a drugstore into a general merchandise enterprise in 1897. Ben Bishop had a wagon shop in the earliest times and was assisted by Charlie and Dave

Dr. J. A. Parkinson of Riceville in 1900. Note the produce on his wagon which he has received as payment.

Boyd, the latter a well-known blacksmith for over 65 years. Charlie Boyd gained fame as an inventor of a variety of tools and machines. Bill Vaughn operated a tanyard, and his son, along with the Vincent family, gained a name for creating fine furniture.

Although relatively small since its incorporation in 1911, with H. A. Collins as the first chairman of the city commission, Niota has always been considered a well-established and progressive town. The persons who have come to be of significant influence in the Niota community since the turn of the century have inevitably risen to places of importance in the county and, in fact, in the state as a whole.

Niota began as a station of the ET&G Railroad before the Civil War, known as Mouse Creek. H. L. Schultz developed a community by selling building lots. The first industry of any consequence was a tanyard started by Eli Dixon, Jr. The "Tan Yard" changed hands until 1879 when it became the property of Samuel P. Blair. By this time, the community had grown and

The Mouse Creek/Niota depot in 1905. Pictured here, from left, are H. B. Burn; J. L. (Jack) Burn; W. A. Burn; J. L. (Jim) Burn, Depot Agent; James P. Lewis; and John I. Forrest (on horse).

boasted of one of the best-known educational institutions in the area, Mouse Creek Academy.

Blair is also remembered for his aid in establishing the Cumberland Presbyterian Church in Niota. The casting of a church bell was always significant, and Blair, with three others, paid for this undertaking. The names of the "Four Bs" were inscribed on the bell: Blair, Brock, Buttram, and Burnes. It is ironic, given the important role that the Burn family played in the history of the community, that the bell makers incorrectly spelled their name on this artifact that now hangs in the Methodist Church steeple.

Unfortunately, Blair eventually experienced financial disaster. In 1913, in a foreclosure sale, most of his Niota holdings were bought by James L. Burn and W. F. Forrest for the Crescent Hosiery Mill which they had organized to give employment to members of the growing community.

The Crescent mill became a central fixture of the community.

The first stockholders included several members of the Burn family, Forrest, J. C. Cate, T. J. Isbell, and H. M. and R. S. Willson. H. M. Willson became the first president and J. L. Burn was the vice-president. W. L. Forrest managed it until the 1930s. In later years Hugh Willson, grandson of H. M. Willson, became the head of the Citizens National Bank, a thriving institution in the county. The Forrest family name was carried on by the J. Ben Forrest Hardware and Furniture Company. The family of the first city commission chairman, H. A. Collins, became involved in a successful feedstore and the advancement of education in the community.

The other central fixture in the community's growth and development has been the Bank of Niota. In fact, *Dun and Bradstreet* (1920) described the village as "a banking town." The bank was organized the same year that the town was incorporated. J. L. Burn served as the first president and H. M. Willson was the vice-president. C. B. Staley became cashier in 1913 and remained with the bank until his death in 1971.

Niota provides a good example of one aspect of the development of many communities throughout the nineteenth and early twentieth centuries—fires. Because of the lack of water systems, it was not uncommon for fires to destroy important buildings and to devastate entire towns. Niota seems to have had more than its share. The entire business section burned in 1897, another fire destroyed a major business in 1910, and a section of the business district was again destroyed in the late 1920s. As late as 1966, fire continued to play havoc with the town when its major industry, Crescent Mill, burned.

Athens experienced the same disasters time and again. Many citizens can recall the Red Elephant Fire, the first high school fire in the late 1940s, the loss of the original Keith Memorial Methodist Church, the second high school fire in the 1950s, and the burning of the beautifully restored and meticulously remodeled county court house in 1964.

To return to Niota, the way that its name was determined is intriguing. Originally called "Mouse Creek," there was continual

The county courthouse after its remodeling and before it was destroyed by fire

confusion of mail and freight with a "Mossy Creek," present-day Jefferson City. When ice cream for a local celebration ended up melting on the loading dock at Mossy Creek something had to be done. According to James Burn, a local railroad agent had suggested "Movilla" since the Morse code station call letter "MO" would not have to be changed. Several local citizens sent their ideas to the railroad superintendent; John Boggess's suggestion was included just as the train to carry the dispatch envelope arrived. Boggess's suggestion of Niota, which was supposedly the name of an Indian chief in a novel he was reading, was selected. Burn also recalls that the original pronunciation was "Nee-o-tah."

Niota became the social center for the entire county with the establishment of Springbrook Golf and County Club which, for many years, was the only facility of its sort in the area. The country club has continued to be the center of the social and recre-

The Etowah YMCA Building as it stood in the early 1900s to welcome the influx of railroaders

ational activities of the county's business, professional, and political leaders.

Etowah came into existence because of the L&N Railroad. The railroad at first had tried to purchase lands for major shops and a terminal at both Tellico Junction and Wetmore but, failing to do so, it ultimately bought nearly 1500 acres from the farms of Joseph Cobb, James L. Cooper, William Paris, William T. Peck, Robert Reynolds, and Robert Smith for $20 per acre. News of the creation of a new town immediately brought an influx of businessmen from all over the South. Soon the whole area was alive with activity; by April 8, 1909, when the town was chartered, it had officially taken up the railroad construction crew's name of "Etowah" (meaning "muddy waters").

The town was laid out in a grid pattern with avenues named for states running north and south, and numbered streets running at right angles to them. The first construction became Tennessee Avenue and this thoroughfare, joined with U.S. Highway

Tennessee Avenue in Etowah immediately after the L&N established the town. The arrow designated the famed "Blue Front."

411, has become the main business district. The first businesses were established to take care of the construction crews and later railroad workers. John Rains put up a small shanty near the new tracks which served as both a store and Etowah's first post office. J. N. Lewis, who had operated a store at Grady three miles north on the L&N, moved to Etowah with the new tracks and became a leading businessman. *The Etowah Enterprise,* an excellent publication later edited by Frank McKinney, was first published on January 5, 1907.

The first major businesses that involved large-scale construction were the hotel-boarding houses that sprang up throughout the town—the Ownbey Boarding House, the Carlock Hotel, the Risk Hotel, the Glenora Hotel (named for Glen Froneberger and Ora Nichols, daughters of the first owners), the Hotel Stafford, the Mountain View Hotel, and the Tennessee Hotel. The Hotel Stafford outlasted all the others. The L&N YMCA was a landmark from 1908 until 1929; it was the site of all kinds of community affairs from town meetings to evangelistic rallies. The Glenora Hotel was distinguished because of its cigar factory. "Glenora Cigars" were made by N. G. Dixon.

The first general store was opened by Lewis' partner, O. L. Davis, and was followed by similar stores run by E. A. Adams, McKinney Brothers, M. M. and H. H. Miller, Reed Brothers, and H. D. Rule and Company. A J. C. Penney Company store came later. A store called "The Blue Front" became one of the best known locations in the city. It was an extremely important meeting place for the community, and several churches and fraternal groups were organized and met there.

Other early businesses included: a furniture store, Sterchi Brothers and Tillery, which arose from the partnership of the Knoxville-based furniture company and J. M. Tillery; Carl Center and N. C. Powell's hardware store; O. A. Rule Furniture Company; and Cunningham and Watts Livery. Hugh Manning established the Gem Theatre (later the Martin) in 1918, and stayed to become one of the leading citizens in the town's early history.

P. A. Kinser opened the first drugstore in Etowah, which later became Gem Drugs, Charles E. McConkey moved from Monroe County in 1908 to organize Etowah Drugs, and B. M. Tallent Drugs opened in 1923. Frank Rutledge came to town in 1909 from Tullahoma to work in the Etowah Bank and Trust Company; he later established an insurance company and the Etowah Water and Light Company. Alex Adams and his son, Stacy, opened an early men's store.

Lawmen were also needed, and following S. H. Vandivere, who was known as the "town marshall," several law officers have become noteworthy. Foremost among these are Burch E. Biggs, who also became an influential political figure in the history of Polk County, and C. O. (Bull) Kennedy. Otto Kennedy, his brother, also became a well-known law officer.

Hardly any business could have taken better advantage of a "boom town" environment than a lumber company. R. L. Tucker established the Etowah Lumber Company in 1910, which was later sold to the Cantrells, helping to make them one of the most influential families in town. Their banking and political interests, particularly those of Paul Cantrell, lent them particular importance.

Because of the sudden influx of railroaders and businessmen, Free Masonry played an important role in the town. By the late 1920s, there were more than half a dozen Masonic bodies and an extremely active chapter of the Order of Eastern Star. At one time Etowah had the largest Masonic membership for a town of its size in the entire nation. M. L. Bryan served as the first worshipful master of the Etowah lodge, and Retta Bryan, his wife, was the first worthy matron of the Order of Eastern Star.

A number of well-known names in Etowah's history have been those of attorneys. The first permanent lawyer was Eugene Ivins who was the first city attorney. The Ivins' name has long been important, with Dan Ivins having served as town recorder for many years. D. W. Lillard, a hero of World War I, came from Decatur to practice for several years. Donald Todd, who would ultimately establish Green Hill Cemetery, came to the city in 1910 to practice law.

A large number of local youngsters became attorneys and established their practices in the city. These included Shields Cagle, William M. Dender, Sam Gilreath, C. B. Stanberry, Amzy Steed (who later became general counsel for the Texaco Oil Corporation), and Knox and Nell Williams. Cousins Ralph Duggan and Tom Taylor established practices in Athens and both became important following World War II.

Two of the first physicians in Etowah were W. R. Froneberger and J. O. Nichols. They were keen businessmen and, in addition to their medical practice, each established a drugstore—the Gem and Rexall respectively—and jointly established a hotel. Other early physicians were H. E. Center, E. M. Foreman, and Olin Rogers. Early dentists were E. M. Akins, G. L. Keith, W. S. Moore, and L. C. Ogle. W. R. Anderson and E. R. Battle later came to town and practiced for many years.

Not until 1929 did Etowah get its first hospital. Dr. P. E. Parker from Sweetwater built a two-story hospital on Fifth Street which did well until the Depression when it closed. Dr. Spenser McClary, who had moved his practice to Etowah in

1925, reopened the hospital in 1935. He and his son, Boyd, operated it until the beginning of World War II when Boyd entered the service and his father died.

Upon his return from the war Boyd McClary, with Homer Johnson and others, began to seek funds for a modern hospital in Etowah. Their dream and dedicated work finally were successful in 1965 when the Hill-Burton Act funded the construction of the Woods Memorial Hospital. The hospital was named for the parents of George Woods, a local political leader who had been instrumental in procuring the funds that were finally approved for the building project.

One important community landmark is the city library. The Carnegie Foundation offered grants before the second world war for the establishment of free public libraries in new communities such as Etowah. A group of citizens including T. A. Abner, A. B. Bayless, C. D. Bevan, N. Z. Dewees, John M. Johnson, and Haywood York obtained a grant that resulted in Etowah's having the only Carnegie Library in southeast Tennessee. Until 1922, while a new educational plant was being constructed, the local high school held classes in the library.

In many respects, Etowah is still a young town, not yet close to a centennial celebration. Many of the old buildings that orginally constituted the business district still stand, and there seems to be a community spirit of preservation that has been lacking elsewhere in the county. Many beautiful homes still stand along tree-lined avenues—sometimes like a scene from some idealized past. One can only imagine what Etowah might have been like today had the Depression not occurred and the L&N not decided against reequipping the wood-car repair shops to repair metal cars.

The Black Community

Unfortunately not much attention has been paid to the development of the black community in the county and much information has been lost. While that which is recalled here is certainly incomplete, it is fortunate that a central figure of the black community of the county, Professor W. E. Nash, was still alive at the time of this writing. Not only are Professor Nash's recollections an important source of historical information, but his own life story is a high light of the county's history.

Nash was born in Lunenburg County, Virginia in 1887; by the time he was eight he had been hired out by his mother as a waterboy carrying water to field hands working on large farms. The first year that he worked he earned his food and a few clothes; the second year, he earned $9 and $12 the third. By the time he was sixteen, he was earning $40 a year, and had begun to drive freight wagons.

Nash had always had a desire, encouraged by his mother, to get an education. Undaunted by what many might consider a late start, he left home in 1905 with $11 and two pairs of pants, walked 20 miles to Chase City, Virginia, and entered school. Working at whatever jobs were available, he completed high school when he was 27. He returned to his home where a group of parents and community leaders agreed to start a private school with Nash as the teacher. Each of the 50 students paid 50¢ a month—at that time, $25 a month was good pay for a teacher in many areas.

In less than a year, a local Presbyterian group decided that it would be a good idea to grant a scholarship to some deserving youth to attend Knoxville College, and chose Nash. He sold a tobacco crop and a calf, and with his belongings carried in a small "telescope" case, set out for Knoxville. There he worked on campus helping tutor the younger students. He was so valuable to the college that when the U.S. entered World War I the president of the institution got him exempted from the draft to stay at the school and work. In 1921, following his graduation, Nash came to Athens to be assistant to J. L. Cook at the Athens Academy. Nash knew Booker T. Washington personally, having met him at religious and educational functions, and was greatly influenced by him.

When Nash arrived, there were black persons in their 80s and 90s who had been among the first to come to the county. Blacks had originally come into the county either with the settlers, or as a result of being purchased at "slave sales" up until the time of the Civil War. By the 1800s, few—if any—slaves came to this immediate area directly from Africa. Virginia had come to be known as the "slave breeding ground," and most major cities in that state had periodic sales in which the slaves were sold at auction.

The slaveowners usually attended the auctions together, and marched the slaves back to their new homes in groups. East Tennessee was a major route south toward Atlanta. If someone became ill or could not make the full trip, he would be sold, traded, or given away along the route. In this way, less affluent people might acquire one or two slaves across several years. "Slaves" in this situation simply meant an additional hand to work beside the slaveowners in their fields and mills. The huge sprawl of cotton fields, with hundreds of field hands and their overseers spread out across a vast acreage, was unknown in McMinn County. At the height of slavery, there were only a small number of persons in the county owning more than half a dozen slaves.

Nash stressed that, the general cruelties of the slavery period notwithstanding, the stories he had heard indicated that relations between the races were peaceful and harmonious most of the time. People were respected for the quality of their work—a hard worker who was trustworthy and dependable was considered a useful member of the community regardless of color. Slothfulness of any color was, on the other hand, despised. Throughout the middle 1900s an environment was being created that would allow for movement towards equality in the 1960s.

Four of the best-known black citizens who were still alive in the early 1920s were Rose Baker, Isaac Matlock, George Gettys, and William Keith. As the names suggest, the freed slaves assumed the surnames of their former masters, and thus the same names are handed down in the black community that are found in the white community. The names were typically preceded by the respectful designations "Aunt" and "Uncle" which came to be scorned by later generations. Mrs. Baker had been a slave; she was an active community leader and one of the first members of the Cumberland Presbyterian Church (Freedman's Chapel).

Matlock was known for his gardening abilities; Keith was a drayman delivering freight from the Southern depot.

Another old citizen was Pat Spriggs, who gained some degree of notoriety because of an event that had occurred during the Civil War. Spriggs, like several other young black men from the area, served in Sherman's army, campaigned in East Tennessee, and participated in the "March to the Sea." One night near Atlanta, the cry arose about two in the morning that camp must be broken and a forced march immediately begun. In his haste, Spriggs did not have time to pull on his socks. Evidently a morning of marching and a day of fighting without socks left a deep impression, for until he died in 1930, Spriggs never slept a single night without wearing his socks.

Finally, in this early period, mention should be made of Bart Arnwine. Arnwine had three trademarks—a broad sense of humor, a shining, double-bladed ax, and the reputation of being able to thresh more wheat in one day than anyone in the county. Like several of these memorable people, Arnwine lived to be over 100 years old.

Nash recalled many blacks who made important contributions between 1921 and 1953, when he was involved in the county's educational system. C. H. Wilson, the last principal of the Athens Academy, was for 50 years the minister of the United Presbyterian Church. Walt Dotson operated the first black funeral establishment and was an active Mason in the highly thought of Black Masonic Order in Athens. Bill Scheeler was a railroad man and a minister. Reuben Scheeler, for nine years a teacher at Cook High School, went on to West Virginia State, Alabama State, and Southern University. He later worked with immigration officials in Texas.

Brice Buchanan was active in political, civic, and church affairs, and for many years was the much-beloved janitor at McMinn County High School. For many students across the years his desk in the basement boiler room was a place of genuine friendliness, advice, and mutual respect that knew no racial lines.

Burkett Witt was also active in a broad spectrum of community concerns. He became popular as a chef operating various establishments in Athens and the surrounding area beginning in the early 1950s. He then became active in community politics, serving several terms as city councilman. In 1983 he was elected mayor of Athens, the first black person to serve in such a capacity in the entire region.

Nash also remembered the efforts of Arthur Fergerson, Sr., an AME minister; Teresa Wilson, a loving teacher; and Horace King, who was a mathematical genius, a meteorological specialist for the government in World War II, and a successful textbook author and professor at Riverside, California, Junior College.

Professor Nash's recollections of notable blacks can be reinforced by others mentioned by J. M. Sharp. In addition to George Gettys, James Gettys owned a second slave named Uncle Nelse. When James Gettys fell on hard times, he was forced to sell Nelse. He was purchased by the Reverend Edwin Atlee, who did not believe in slavery, but was a friend of Gettys. Atlee immediately arranged a job going through the area buying poultry and eggs so that Nelse could buy his freedom.

On one trip into Rhea County Nelse was brought to the sheriff to be whipped because "he was too big for a negro." The sheriff, a man named Allen, resigned his position instead of whipping the kindly gentleman. A local minister stepped in and carried out the task. Although the Civil War came before the debt was paid, Nelse stayed with Atlee until it was paid in full. He later, with his wife, was responsible for taking in and raising the orphan boy, J.L. (Jake) Cook.

Sharp also mentions the following persons: Berry and Tish Isbell; the Reverend Amos Jackson, whose favorite saying was "I had a kind master (R. C. Jackson), but I love my freedom—if I forget thee, O Republican Party, let my tongue cleave to the roof of my mouth and my right hand forget her cunning"; the Reverend Jacob Armstrong who was popular in both black and white camp meetings; Roger Sherman, a mechanic; George Henderson, a bricklayer; Peter Wilds and Dick Branum, draymen; and Will Matlock and Albert Evans, barbers.

The key figure of the period after 1953 for the entire black community was Harper Johnson who was born near Riceville, and with his family moved to Athens in the 1920s. He attended the J. L. Cook High School, where he distinguished himself in the classroom and on the athletic field. Upon graduation, he attended Morristown Junior College, and then returned to teach in the black schools of Etowah for twelve years. During this time, Johnson completed his education and returned to Cook High as a teacher and coach. In 1953, when Professor Nash retired, he became principal.

In many respects, Harper Johnson represented a mentality that was beginning to come of age, a new consciousness of human dignity that was arising among black persons across the South. Until integration occurred in the mid-1960s, Johnson was an uncompromising voice calling for equality and justice. His students must have new textbooks and new desks, just like the white students. He was a reasonable man who desired to bring about integration in a way that would insure a common foundation on which to build after the dramatic changes that would have to occur had taken place. Johnson became to his generation of students, as Nash had been to the preceding one, the model who would challenge young blacks to strive for only the highest that their lives could attain. He was in every way an uncommon man for an uncommon time, and the respect that was necessary for integration to work beyond just the surface changes that the law demanded was generated by his decisiveness and leadership.

Johnson moved to Nashville in the late 1960s where he worked for the Tennessee Education Association. To honor him, the TEA began to give the E. Harper Johnson Human Relations Award. Significantly, two of these awards have been presented to McMinn Countians—the first, to Professor Nash, and the second to J. Neal Ensminger, the executive editor of *The Daily Post-Athenian*. Harper Johnson's influence on every aspect of life in the county is high. He will always be considered one of the "shapers" of the county's destiny. He died in 1982.

Professor Nash concluded his reminiscences by giving attention to his thoughts for the future of the black community of the county. He was quick with a response that was undoubtedly already well-formed in his mind: "If the young people can continue to have ambition and some goal, and do not begin to have an inferiority complex, the future will be bright." One wonders if these sentiments might not apply to the entire county as it moves into a future where its special uniqueness competes with a much larger and much more complex "global village." To touch base with some old sources of wisdom is both refreshing and hopeful.

Religion

A general overview of American religious history can be given quickly. Following the Revolutionary War and the expansion beyond the Appalachians, religion moved immediately to the new frontier. With this movement, the character of religion in America underwent a drastic change. Instead of the staid, intellectual approach that had characterized religion on the eastern seaboard, the religion of the new frontier was charged with the same highly emotional spirit that paralleled the adventuresome pioneer mentality and the daring that transformed the old wilderness areas. By 1800 a revivalist movement was in full swing. Through two "Great Awakenings" and across the better part of two centuries, in many respects, the county's religious preferences have changed very little.

McMinn County was in the heart of the revival movement. Throughout the early period the county was a central place for the first camp meetings and "brush arbors" in southeastern Tennessee that gave the great revivals, and flaming tongued orators who stood in their midst, their memorable flavor.

The first denomination to come to the frontier were the Presbyterians. They were the strongest group on the seaboard and worked from a well-established organization. However, there were immediate problems. The Presbyterians believed in Calvinist doctrines of predestination and placed little or no emphasis on the free will of the human being. But the frontier character had been forged in the caldron of human will, leading to a conflict too great for the old traditions to bear. A major split within the denomination produced the "Cumberland Presbyterians" who softened the old Calvinism. This new group grew significantly and was well-represented in the county.

The Baptist movement into the area followed on the heels of the first revival activities. The Baptists succeeded quickly and got off to a much better start than the Presbyterians for at least three reasons. First, they were not bound by old traditions, and second, they had a theology that stressed free will. Finally, they had ministers who were close to the people, typically being lay persons who felt "called to preach" and performed ministerial activities in addition to their regular work.

Unfortunately, the Baptists soon became hamstrung on theological issues. Early in the 1800s, the "Landmarkism" controversy erupted over the belief that certain biblical "landmarks" were being compromised by theological liberals. Then, in the late 1840s, disagreement over the slavery question fostered a split that divided the Baptist faith in the United States into the Southern and American Baptist Conventions. Since that time all Baptist congregations in the county, with the exception of random "independent" Baptist groups which have appeared from time to time, have belonged to the Southern Baptist Convention.

The most successful early religious activitites were Methodist. The "circuit riders" were trained in the scriptures, well-disciplined as a group, and unbelievably energetic in covering the wide countryside. The Methodists, having established structured conferences to provide direction and supervision, were also well-organized.

It was not until the Civil War period that divisions led to the organization of the Methodist Episcopal Church, South. Every one of the Holston Conference ministers agreed with the "Plan of Separation," and thus any divisions were held at a minimum. Many of the political and social leaders of the eastern part of the state, like "Parson" Brownlow, were Methodist. The divisions elsewhere which created groups like the Republican Methodist Church, the Wesleyan Connection, and the Methodist Protestant Church were of little consequence in McMinn County.

Although the real strength of Methodism may be in the northern part of the Holston Conference between Knoxville and southwestern Virginia, the impact on McMinn County has been immense. This has been especially true because of the presence of Tennessee Wesleyan College and Hiwassee College in nearby Madisonville. Families of every denomination have been touched by these schools, and their graduates have typically become the leading citizens of the communities in the area.

Limitations of time and space preclude lengthy accounts of the churches in the county. All are distinctive and became the focal points of town and country life. What will be given here is, at best, a representative sketch of some of the earliest churches which have continuous histories into the present.

The first religious experiences in the county were the old camp meetings which grew out of the great revivals. The most important of these were located at Cedar Springs, Spring Creek, and South Liberty. People came from great distances and spent a few days or weeks studying and worshipping—and socializing—in the highly spiritualized atmosphere of the camps.

The first church to be organized in the county was the Calhoun Methodist Church in 1819. It was also the first church in the Cleveland District of the Holston Conference. The old church building stood as a historical landmark until the late 1960s. Its remaining graveyard is, beyond doubt, the most intriguing in the county. An early attempt to establish a Presbyterian Church at Calhoun was short-lived in spite of the assistance of Governor Joseph McMinn. A Baptist Church was established in 1874.

There is some debate as to which was the next church to be organized. More than likely that honor belongs to what was called "The Baptist Church of Christ at Big Springs on the Little Mouse Creek." This was in 1822, and like most of the churches in the county, it was organized in a home—that of Elijah Hurst. One of the charter members was Jacob Womac, a leader of the Watauga Association, the political ancestor of the state of Tennessee. Another charter member was Isaac Lane, who had fought at King's Mountain and brought a large family to live in the Mouse Creek area. This church was closed about the time of the Civil War. In 1885 some former members established the Mouse Creek

Mars Hill Presbyterian Church in Athens

Baptist Church. Eventually, the name was changed to the First Baptist Church of Niota.

The Zion Hill Baptist Church was also organized in 1822. Although it is a small rural church today, in that period it was of great importance. Many churches in the county grew out of Zion Hill, not the least of which was First Baptist in Athens. Several of the most important Baptist ministers in the county's early history were associated with Zion Hill and its parent church, Chestua Baptist in Monroe County, including Daniel Buckner who was named for his father's close friend Daniel Boone, Thomas and James Russell, and J. P. Kefauver, grandfather of Estes Kefauver.

The oldest church in Athens is the Mars Hill Presbyterian Church, which was organized in 1823. Among the first members were the Andersons, Breazeales, Bridges, Dixsons, Gettys, Jacksons, Keys, McKeldins, Neils, Popes, Reids, and Wilsons. During the Civil War the church separated from the Northern Presbytery and even allowed its minister to serve the Southern cause as a chaplain. The structure itself, originally built by the Cleages, has been rebuilt, remodeled, and survived fire to become one of the most beautiful buildings in the county.

In 1824 the First Baptist Church was formed. Its original building was a log structure made available by a local physician and located on the site of the present Cedar Grove Cemetery.

In 1889 the congregation erected a new building near the right front of the present structure. In 1941 Charles Stephen Bond led in a building project at the present site, where the home of R. J. Fisher had been located. Under the leadership of R. Richard Smith, the present sanctuary was completed in 1967. For many years this has been the largest church in the county. The First Baptist Church established three missions that later became important churches in their own right: East Athens Baptist Church in the Morningside community, West End Baptist Church in the Layman Hill area, and Central Baptist Church in the Avalon Heights section.

In 1825 the Methodist Episcopal Church was established on property across Washington Avenue from the present site of Foree Clinic; the designation "South" was added on the eve of the Civil War. In 1829 Brownlow was the minister. A second building was in use from 1851 until 1878, when one of the most beautiful churches in the region was built. On Christmas night, 1947, one of the most spectacular fires in the city's history completely destroyed this building, which had been named "Keith Memorial" in 1939. The congregation met in the local high school for two years, constructed the present building, and has enjoyed steady growth ever since.

St. Paul's Episcopal Church began services in 1834. The graceful lines of the present building on South Jackson Street serve as a fitting tribute to the devotion of the typically small congregations that have kept the Episcopalian faith alive in the county.

The present Trinity Methodist Church, whose members held primarily Northern sympathies, was not formed until after the Civil War in 1865. Originally named the First Methodist Episcopal Church, and after worshipping at several locations, the growing congregation entered the present structure in 1910; the site had been the well-known Foster's Livery Stable. The church has been closely associated with the life of Tennessee Wesleyan College over the years. A building on campus memorializes two of its ministers, John Petty and John Manker. The most famous minister was Nathaniel Green Taylor, who served at one time in the United States House of Representatives. His two sons, Robert Love and Alfred A., became governors of the state.

The Taylor story is one of the most famous in Tennessee history. Bob was a Democrat and Alf a Republican. Since they were "roses from the same garden," their campaign came to be known, with reference to the old feud between the houses of York and Lancaster, as "The War of the Roses." The men's humor, skilled oratory, and musical ability turned out campaign crowds numbering in the tens of thousands. Bob's campaign song was "Dixie" and Alf's "Yankee Doodle." Bob won by a narrow majority, eventually served three terms, and went on to be a senator and a representative. Alf then served one term as governor, and three as congressman. Before their deaths, they toured the nation appearing before large audiences as "Yankee Doodle and Dixie."

In 1872, as part of the Brient development northeast of Athens, a church was established at Happy Top. With most of the enterprises of that community, it moved to Tellico Junction in 1893, and was known until 1909 as the Cross Grove Baptist Church. At that time the name of the community was changed to Englewood, and the church became the First Baptist Church. The Methodist Church in Englewood was organized in 1902. One name prominent at this time, which appears time and again in the early organizational activities of many churches in the county, is that of J. R. Land.

The First United Presbyterian Church, U.S.A., which stands on North Jackson Street, across from the Tennessee Wesleyan campus, was erected in 1892. The old church and manse next door stand much as they did in 1902. The church had been established in 1889 by a local man who had returned to Athens after receiving an excellent education. J. L. ("Jake") Cook—with the exception of W. E. Nash and Harper Johnson—is the best-known and most influential black person in the county's history. The present pastor, Charles Johnson, who has held this position since 1966, is the longest standing member of the present clergy in the county and is a prominent black leader.

Cook's parents had been slaves of one of the earliest settlers, Judge J. B. Cooke, but died when Jake was a young child. He was raised by "Uncle Nelse" and "Aunt Huldy" Gettys who had been slaves for the Gettys family. He was an avid student, and from the public schools he went on to Fisk University and then Knoxville College where he graduated in 1888. He then graduated from Alleghany Theological Seminary in Pennsylvania, and returned in 1891 to establish the "Academy of Athens." This school quickly gained recognition as one of the best black schools in the South.

Cook was the only black at the national convention of the Presbyterian Church in Omaha in 1898. His talk was described in a publication of that day, *The Christian Instructor,* as "the brightest and most popular address delivered before the Assembly....Mr. Cook is the best possible object lesson of the value of the work being done by the Board of Missions to the Freedmen."

Cook continued in Athens as head of the academy and minister of the church until 1900 when he became president of Henderson Institute in Henderson, North Carolina. Through the mid-sixties Cook High School commemorated this teacher.

Most of the churches in Etowah started about the same time that the town was established in 1906. There had been churches in the surrounding area, and the old Cane Creek campground operated by the Methodists was nearby. There was a great deal of competition among young suitors at Foster's Livery Stable for buggies and teams to drive to the camp meetings. Near the area that became Etowah was Crittenden Fork Baptist Church, later called Goodsprings. It was organized in 1872 and has always been one of the strongest rural churches in the county. The Coghill Baptist Church was organized even earlier, in 1860, south of the Etowah area near the present Polk County line. The first minister, E. C. Denton, served the church for 25 years. The church was one of the first before 1900 to begin the process of "mission" efforts to start new churches by organizing the Wetmore Baptist Church at Wetmore Station.

The Wesleyanna Methodist Church was organized in 1861. In its long history, the church has been served by over 70 ministers, 38 of whom have gone on to become bishops.

The Foster Livery Stable about 1910, where Trinity Methodist Church now stands

The oldest congregation in Etowah is the present Wesley Memorial Methodist Church. It was formerly the Tenth Street Methodist Church, and before that the Methodist Episcopal Church, South. It was instituted in 1906 and was the only church building in Etowah for over a year; many of the other congregations in town met in this building or at the old "Blue Front" on Tennessee Avenue.

Three of the main churches in Etowah today started in 1907–1908, and each met for some time at the "Blue Front." The First Baptist Church showed the largest growth, and by 1919 had one of the largest Sunday schools in all of East Tennessee. Among the charter members were names that come down to the present—Cantrell, Creasman, Riggs, Roylston, Tillery, and Williams. W. H. Runion was the first minister, and for several years there was a series of building projects. Under the 11-year pastorate of Dr. A. F. Mahan the church membership grew to over 1000. In later years, E. M. Holt led the church to great success, and today the newly constructed sanctuary is one of the most beautiful in the county.

St. Paul's was the third Methodist Church to be formed in Etowah. For 19 years the members worshipped on Pennsylvania Avenue. J. W. May was the first minister, and among the early members were M. L. Bryan, D. H. Day, Charlie Hutsell, John Reed, and Oran Reed. In 1926 the congregation moved to the Georgia Avenue and Eighth Street site. Mars Hill Methodist Church (built on a hill property owned by Benny Mars) was organized in 1906.

The First Presbyterian Church was organized in June 1908. The charter members were J. A. Fowler, Mrs. Horace Green, P. A. Kinser, G. D. Pate, Mrs. D. M. Pearson, W. C. Reynolds, and Charles Wagner.

Important information remains that could fill many volumes, but space limitations here are severe. Men such as Dillard Brown and Henry Stamey came out of Clearwater Baptist to become well-known leaders. Women such as Gussie Rose List lovingly taught a whole generation of Athenians to sing, and Mrs. Ruth Sharp's Sunday school class grew into Allen Memorial Methodist Church. Mount Harmony Baptist Church in 1947 was acknowledged as the most outstanding rural church in the state. Jesse Dodson had a long and influential pastorate at Eastanallee Baptist. Liberty Hill Church of Christ was used during the Civil War as a "pest house" for soldiers with contagious diseases. Churches have a place of honor in the county's history.

Education

Education has always been a central concern in the county. The first educational institutions were mission schools for the Indians which were provided by various religious organizations with the ostensive purpose of education, but perhaps primarily concerned with evangelism. The Indians did not particularly care for the religion of the whites, but they appreciated educational opportunity sometimes even more than the majority of the first pioneers who gave priority to the children helping with the work in the new settlement. The mission to the Cherokees enjoyed great success until the time of the removal.

The Methodists established a school called "The Conasauga Mission," while a Presbyterian group operating from Maryville under a pioneer missionary named Gideon Blackburn started a school at Walker's Ferry. Return Meigs, the capable Indian agent for the area, did a great deal to advance education among those under his charge, and in later years served on the board of trustees for Forest Hill Academy.

Frontier children learned the "three Rs" at their mothers' knees. As the settlers prospered the more affluent employed young men with college backgrounds to tutor their children; educated ministers also served as teachers. Frequently the children of less fortunate neighbors were invited to join the educational activities. As early as 1805, for example, there are records of George Barber Davis who taught for the John Rogers' family at Rogers' Creek. Davis later moved to the mission school at Walker's Ferry.

Beginning about 1823 at least two specific types of educational institutions appeared in the county. First, there were private schools called "academies." Then, to a lesser extent, there were the first instances of public, or "free," education. In addition, itinerant teachers travelled the countryside establishing "schools" in private dwellings or renting space for various lengths of time from a few weeks to several months.

The "academies" were an intriguing educational enterprise. They were typically secondary schools, but might also cover everything from primary level work to seminary training. Hiwassee Academy in Calhoun was the first in the county. It opened around 1823. Later, it was known as Hiwassee Masonic Institution and, by as late as 1874, had nearly 100 students.

In Athens, the Forest Hill Academy was established in 1825, and it has only been in the most recent years, with the establishment of Westside Elementary School, that the name Forest Hill has not been associated with education in the county. The large Cane Creek Academy or Seminary kept alive the memories of the old Cane Creek Methodist Campground until the middle 1800s.

The Forest Hill Academy in 1907

In 1857 three important academies were established. In Riceville, John Biggs and Mollie Porter opened the Riceville Academy. Ten years later the school was rechartered as the Riceville Scientific and Classical Institute. Dr. N. B. Goforth led the school to excellence. He established monthly public oral examinations, and large crowds would gather to hear the students (often termed "scholars" in the old records) perform. Dr. Goforth left Riceville around 1877 to go to Mossy Creek—present-day Jefferson City—to help establish Newman Female College and to marry the daughter of its founder. This school later became Carson-Newman College.

Two other academies were started this same year in Mouse Creek (Niota). Because of a conflict over location, one came to be known as Mouse Creek Male and Female Academy, and the other as Fountain Hill Academy. By 1881 A. W. Weeks had established Mount Harmony Select School for Males and Females three miles outside of Mouse Creek. An advertisement from that time emphasized the importance of the location "in the beautiful and healthy valley of the Eastanallee, in a community where the people have long been distinguished for their generosity, strict morality, and harmonious workings for the advancement of education and refinement." The following "terms" were set forth:

Mouse Creek Academy in the late nineteenth century. Note the fly on the upper right corner of the glass plate negative.

> FIRST CLASS—To include Orthography, Reading, Writing, Primary Arithmetic $5.00
> SECOND CLASS—To include English Grammar, Geography, First Lessons in Composition and Practical Arithmetic $7.50

> THIRD CLASS—To include Natural Philosophy,
> U.S. History, Anatomy, and Elementary Algebra $8.75
> FOURTH CLASS—Mental Philosophy, Common School
> Astronomy, Higher Arithmetic, Higher Algebra $10.00
> FIFTH CLASS—Rhetoric and Composition, Chemistry,
> Geometry, Trigonometry, Conic Sections, Analytic Geometry
> and Mathematical Astronomy $15.00
> CONTINGENT FEE—25Cts. to be paid by each student
> on entering school.
>
> Students will be charged from the time they enter school to the close of the term. Deductions made only in case of protracted sickness. Board, including lights, can be had in good families at cheap rates. Students wishing to board themselves can obtains rooms and fuel for a trifle.

The names of the trustees indicate family ties that have been important across the years: J. N. Cate, W. H. Forrest, D. P. Isbell, James Lewis (chairman), J. D. Lowry, Jr., J. P. Netherland, E. M. Stalcup, and W. P. Willson.

Elementary or primary education began in an organized manner in 1823. Under Presbyterian guidance, a log building was erected in the present Cedar Grove Cemetery and was known as Cedar Grove School. Other schools at this early time were the Glover School, where McMinn Dodson taught, the Gum Hill School, and the Eastanallee School. Drawing from an old record, Ozelle Powers vividly describes the latter:

> The school was built on a section of land that had been worn out and no longer used for farming. The building was made of logs and had a rough pine floor of split logs. It had two doors, one on each side, and had four windows, one on each side of the doors. The building was approximatley twenty feet by twenty feet. At one end of the building was a rock fire place which was used for heating. The children had split logs for seats. The children studied aloud, and the teacher believed in the hickory stick. The length of the school term was about six weeks and during this time the children went to school from sun-up to sun-down.

The first public schools were not adequately financed, and sometimes were referred to as "pauper schools." Even though an act was passed by the state legislature in 1873 to establish a public school system, a local option school tax was defeated. In 1874 there were 66 schools and 73 teachers in the county. They taught approximately three months out of the year, and were paid $30.00 per month.

The public school situation had deteriorated to such an extent by 1878 that they appeared to be on the brink of extinction. Superintendent C. R. Hoyl, in a report to the state superintendent, begged for help: "Oh, God! for Christ's sake forbid it, I would humbly pray thee, in His name, Amen!"

There was also keen competition between the public and private schools. Lydia Bridges had the most prestigious private school in the area. It met in the basement of the Bridges' Hotel and was supported by the leading families of the community. Her students were derided as "Cellar Bugs" by the public school students who were, in turn, called "Gully Bugs" because of the location of their school near the large gully which ran near the north side of the school and along the south side of the town square.

When Athens was incorporated in 1903 taxes could be levied and a city school system established. For the first six years the old Forest Hill Academy was used. Then in 1909 the present Forest Hill building, much of which has now been torn down, was constructed. Later, a school as added in North Athens, and after World War II schools were added in the Ingleside and City Park sections of the expanding town. Men like Bob Benton, George Galloway, and Harold Powers will remain important in the history of elementary education in the area. W. F. Whitaker was the superintendent during the period of greatest growth.

Up until the early part of the twentieth century there was little or no emphasis placed on educating the black population. A few attempts made by white teachers from the North were met by strong resistance. At least four black schools were burned. In 1926 the county, with the help from the city and the Rosenwald Foundation, established a comprehensive black school called the Athens Training School. It was later renamed Cook High School in honor of J. L. Cook and, with other black schools in the Etowah area, operated until the desegregation period of the mid-

1960s. The Cook school was an outgrowth of the "Academy of Athens" mentioned earlier which had been located at the top of Depot Hill on the Wilson property next to Laycock Funeral Home.

In 1891 a secondary school law was passed. Two years later, the county purchased the property of the old Athens Female College from Dr. L. L. H. Carlock for $2500. On April 20, 1893, McMinn County High School was opened as the first public secondary school in East Tennessee and the second in the entire state. The first principal was M. R. M. Burke. In recent years, the work of B. L. Hale and J. Will Foster has been most noteworthy.

High schools slowly became established in the other large communities, such as the one housed for a time in the Carnegie Library in Etowah. These were smaller, but built up records of proud accomplishment. After a series of consolidations since the mid-1960s there are now only two high schools, McMinn High in its new structure on Congress Parkway in Athens, and McMinn Central between Etowah and Englewood on Highway 411.

The story of education in McMinn County is incomplete without a sketch of Tennessee Wesleyan College. Before 1850 a private academy had existed at the present site of the college, but it had burned. The Odd Fellows Lodge, whose members helped to start several colleges in Virginia and Tennessee, obtained a charter to build a college on the site and started the construction of the building known today as "Old College," which stands at the heart of the campus. Financial problems resulted in the Odd Fellows proposing a joint undertaking with the Methodist Church.

The name Athens Female College was chosen in 1857, and by the time of the Civil War it was a thriving institution. A newspaper advertisement in 1863 read: "The larger and better portion of the young men of the country are in the army, fighting the battles of freedom and independence. And whatever else you leave undone, don't neglect to educate your daughters."

However, financial problems, which have almost always plagued the college, arose again, and additional changes within the Methodist organization altered the character of the college. The Holston Conference of the Methodist Episcopal Church—

the group with Union loyalties—was reorganized in 1865 at Athens. The female college owed a large sum to its president, Dr. Erastus Rowley, and he claimed ownership of the college against those debts. He immediately sold it to the newly reorganized conference, and in 1867 it became known as East Tennessee Wesleyan College. A year later it became coeducational and was renamed East Tennessee Wesleyan University.

In 1884 Dr. John Fletcher Spence became president and commenced a 26-year administration. During this period the names Grant Memorial University and then U.S. Grant University were used. Under this name it consolidated with the University of Chattanooga and was usually referred to simply as "The Athens School." This consolidation continued until 1925 under the administration of a variety of Chattanooga-based presidents and deans, the most important of whom was Arlo Ayres Brown who went on to be president of Drew University and a leading voice in American education in the first half of the twentieth century.

Perhaps the most important person in the college's history came on the scene in 1918, when James L. Robb began to administer the Athens campus. In 1925, when the separation of the two schools occurred, Robb became president, and the school was named Tennessee Wesleyan College.

Robb's tenure lasted until 1950, and he led the college through a period of great financial problems, the Depression, and two major wars. In spite of all this, the college grew both in facilities and student population. Robb's relationship to the Pfeiffer family of New York City resulted in major contributions that built a library, a girls' dormitory, and a gymnasium, the latter bearing Robb's name. Throughout Robb's administration, the college operated as a two-year junior college.

During the administrations of Leroy Martin and Ralph Mohney, the college experienced continued growth having become a four-year institution in 1955. By the end of Mohney's term, the college budget was well over a million dollars, and the enrollment had increased to over seven hundred students. In 1967 the college granted 100 degrees and added several new faculty.

Like other small denominational schools, however, the college fell on very difficult times in the early 1970s. It was feared that the doors might even be closed. Enrollments at private schools sharply declined across the country; at Tennessee Wesleyan it declined by nearly two-thirds. Thanks to efforts of alumni, friends, the community in general, and the able efforts of President George Naff, the college has survived and the immediate future looks strong.

The story of Tennessee Wesleyan College has been a story of continued perseverance and adaptation. It has faced difficult times again and again but always had the strength of character to find new avenues of service in the light of changing demands. At times the college has seemed like a "community within a community," and its initial Union sympathies may have put it at odds with many in the larger community. The college seems to be accepted more and more as a community resource, however, and a distinct asset in which the town can take great pride. To the extent that the community and the college align themselves as they face the future, the college's life will be assured and that of the community enhanced.

A significant part of the story of the schools in the county is the story of athletics. McMinn County has a strong tradition of prowess on the gridiron, basketball court, and baseball diamond. From the time of the old softball and baseball teams that brought large crowds to Fisher Field to the present exodus to Knoxville on football Saturdays to see "The Big Orange," McMinn Countians have been sports enthusiasts. People are likely to recall sporting events and athletes' names more quickly than those of politicians, ministers, and soldiers. It is impossible to recount all of the anecdotes relating to county athletic heroes and their accomplishments. A "Sports Hall of Fame" has been established for that purpose. The persons cited here are only a representative sample.

Perhaps the most successful athlete from the county was Glenn "Mutt" Knox, who graduated from McMinn County High School in 1938 and then attended Tennessee Wesleyan College for two years. With the encouragement of his coach, Rube McCray, he

An Athens High School football team near the turn of the century

then enrolled at William and Mary where he attained Southern Conference MVP honors in basketball in 1943 and All-Southern honors in football. He went on to play both professional basketball and football and later became a successful automobile dealer in Richmond, Virginia.

J. B. "Ace" Adams is a commanding figure in sports in the county's history. He excelled as a baseball player at the University of Tennessee and Tennessee Wesleyan before going on to coach and serve as athletic director at McMinn County High School in the early 1950s. His teams attained some of the best records and won some of the biggest games in the school's history. Adams was also a member of the famed "Athens Oilers." His son, Joe, has become one of the most outstanding baseball coaches in the state at Bradley County High School.

What "Ace" Adams has been to athletics in Athens, "Buck" Brown has been to sports in Englewood. An exceptional baseball and basketball player whose skilled pitching became his trademark, he served as coach and athletic director at Englewood High and later at the new McMinn Central High School into the early 1970s. Englewood fans also recall Charley Raper and Willard Reid, both well-known baseball players, and Shirley Majors, one of their most memorable football players.

Wayne Grubb came from one of the most famous athletic families in the county, and went on to star at UT from 1958–1960. He gained the honor of being named to the All-Alabama Opponents team in 1960. In one of the most famous games in the history of the university, Tennessee faced eventual national champion Louisiana State and Heisman trophy–winner Billy Cannon in Knoxville on November 7, 1959. With the game at its end, and the score 14–13 in favor of UT, LSU attempted to run Cannon for a two point conversion that would win the game. One of the most celebrated pictures in the history of *Sports Illustrated* magazine shows Grubb at the goal line tackling Cannon and preserving the Tennessee victory. Grubb was joined by fellow Athenian Jim Cartwright on this team.

Bob "Mr. Dirty" Deal was well-known multisport athlete in the second quarter of the 1900s, who came to be best-known as an umpire. Deal infuriated fans and coaches alike, but to the players who came to know him personally, there was no kinder and more caring man. His great interest in athletics certainly helped to raise the county's sporting experiences to higher plateaus. Fans of Etowah athletics also recall the exploits of J. "King" Dunn, Frank Thomas "Fatty" York, and Max Carroll.

The following names will bring back memories for many McMinn Countians: Buenos Baker, Henry "Pie" Barnett, Boyd Coffee, "Big Peanut" Daugherty, Claude "Steel Arm" Dickey, Willard Eaves (a member of the 1938 Duke University Rose Bowl team), Lee Fisher, Reed Halcomb, Rankin Hudson, Hobart "Feets" Jones, Ralph Jordan, David Knox, Glenn "Coot" Lawson, Raymond McKee, Benny Monroe, Phil Pierce, Mike Reynolds, Tommy Samples, "Tip" Smith, David Vestal, and Carter Whitaker.

Newspapers

McMinn County has been fortunate in having excellent newspapers across its history, although there have been papers which have taken opposing views and often been in conflict. The two present papers—*The Etowah Enterprise* and the award-winning *The Daily Post-Athenian*—are prime examples of newspapers committed to keeping their subscribers abreast of the information they need.

The first newspaper was *The Hiwassee and Athens Gazette*, which was started in 1830 by two Rhea Countians, S. M. and J. C. S. Hood. This paper continued until 1833 when it was succeeded by J. M. Brezeale's *Tennessee Journal*. Three other papers established before midcentury were *The Hiwassee Patriot*, *The Athens Courier*, and *The Hiwassee Republican*.

The most significant early newspaper event involved bringing Samuel P. Ivins from New Jersey via Knoxville in 1848 to found *The Athens Post*. The paper was conceived as a propaganda medium to advance the new interest in railroading. Using newspapers for political and business purposes was a typical practice in the mid-1800s. Ivins was successful, and *The Post* built a strong foundation under his direction until the late 1880s.

During the Civil War a Union paper called *The Athens Union Post* came into existence. An opposition paper, *The Athenian*, was immediately established; *The Athenian* survived. In the late 1920s, E. T. Taylor and J. Rollo Emert merged the two papers and published a twice-weekly *Post-Athenian* from the North Jackson location that was used until the 1960s.

For a short time around 1936 Hurst Paul published the *McMinn County Herald*. Taylor was looking for a buyer for his paper, and on March 15 Fred Wankan arrived from Mississippi to survey the possibilities of coming to McMinn County. Wankan wanted to buy both local papers and merge them but could not reach an agreement with Paul. Soon after Wankan's purchase of the *Post-Athenian*, the Paul paper ceased to exist. Within a year, Wankan's paper began to be published daily and the present name, *The Daily Post-Athenian*, was established.

In 1937 Wankan made two acquisitions that raised newspapering to new heights in McMinn County. First, the most modern press available was installed, and was used for twenty years. Then, and most important, Wankan convinced Neal Ensminger

J. Neal Ensminger, executive editor of *The Daily Post-Athenian*

to come to work for the paper. Across the years, Ensminger has worked in every branch of the business from reporter to executive editor—with plenty of experience on the presses to boot. Of greater significance than any particular facet of his work, the spirit of the man has become the spirit of the paper, and *The Daily Post-Athenian* has been recognized repeatedly as one of the most outstanding small town papers in the Southeast.

To pick a representative citizen from all who have lived in the county across the years would be difficult, but it would be a compliment to the county to allow Neal Ensminger to stand in that position. His work with the newspaper, local civic clubs, fund-raising projects, his Sunday school class at Keith Memorial, and his advocacy of Tennessee Wesleyan have affected the lives of countless persons in the region. He represents the best that the county can aspire to, and the excellence of *The Daily Post-Athenian* over the past half-century becomes a fitting tribute to him—a man of gentleness and wisdom whose description of the wind in the top of the mulberry bush is etched on the memory as much as the cadence of his voice and the gleam in his eye. Alongside the other institutions of the county, Ensminger himself is an institution.

Wankan sold the *DPA* in 1939, and two years later it passed into the hands of Lowell F. Arterburn. Arterburn's creative concern with communications not only advanced the paper, but also led to the establishment of the county's first radio station, WLAR. When Arterburn died in 1959 his wife, Helen, who was also a physician, led the paper. In 1962 she sold her interests to a group led by Bob Sykes. One of the better-known writers of the region, Bill Casteel of *The Chattanooga Times*, was reared in Athens and started his career at the *DPA*.

The other major newspaper in the county's history has been *The Etowah Enterprise*. It was established in 1907 by Thomas F. Peck from Madisonville who was in charge of the paper's operation until 1946 when it was sold to a local group and Frank McKinney became editor-publisher. McKinney directed the paper for nearly 30 years. The *DPA* group, led by Sykes, purchased the paper in 1964. For a short time in the early part of the century two other papers appeared in Etowah, *The Etowah New Era* and *The Etowah Post*. For a while a paper called *The McMinn County Herald* was published in Englewood.

Finally, there has been one other newspaper venture of importance in the county. In 1960 Archie Wattenbarger established a weekly called *The Athens Press*. The paper did well, but Wattenbarger's untimely death two years later made it impossible for the paper to continue. A last note should call attention to Daisy Rice Spradling whose reporting for the *Chattanooga Times* and feature writing about social and cultural events in McMinn County made her byline famous throughout the region.

Only a lack of space prohibits some discussion of other institutions and similar organizations which have been important in the county. Some mention should be made, however, of the Browning Circle. Organized as a women's reading group by Mrs. May Noel Moody in 1891, the circle ultimately grew to be the city of Athen's only "public" library. The group named itself after the poet Elizabeth Barrett Browning and took as their motto a line from her work: "We strike out blindly to a mark, believed in, but not seen." Over the years the Browning Circle has made many efforts at civic enrichment in addition to the library.

A Faithful Legacy Through Two Wars

Young men from McMinn County have always responded quickly to their country's call during times of war. Their ancestors had fought at King's Mountain in the Revolutionary War. From the Creek Wars to the Battle of New Orleans, from the Civil War to the Spanish-American conflict, McMinn Countians displayed exceptional valor and patriotism.

Charles F. Keith, Jr., has left an intriguing memoir of the first twentieth-century army unit to be mustered in the county, Company "I" of the Sixth Regiment, National Guard of the state of Tennessee. The date of muster was December 20, 1901. The original group was made up of : James A. Arnwine, John B. Camp, Hershel M. Candler, James F. Cook, Robert C. Cockron, William L. Cook, Affett C. Duff, Harry Dixon, Wiley A. Foster, J. Horace Gauldy, Pat S. Horton, Richard J. Haley, William R. Horton, William O. Hoskins, Marshall J. Keith, Charles F. Keith, Jr., Samuel Kelley, George C. Long, Bruce A. Long, M. Luther Minge, T. Edwin Moody, Clay S. Matlock, Edward A. Meckling, F. O. Mahery, Harvey Melton, James P. Minge, Jr., Thomas F. Neil, W. Boyd Nankiville, Roger L. Owen, Charles H. Prescott, Harry C. Peters, Allen W. Rogers, Fred S. Riddle, William H. Rogers, Robert A. Reed, Claude W. Richardson, Mack W. Smith, Charles M. Sanders, Ben F. Sherlin, William H. Stansel, William C. Steed, William R. Thomas, Jacob T. Tuell, Ralph E. Wattles, Charles F. Walker, and Ollie M. West.

There had been a terrible storm and several men in the county could not make it to the "Old Opera House" on North Jackson Street for the mustering ceremony. A Captain Drewery had come from Chattanooga to be in charge and would not be outdone by the elements. He simply took local citizens who were there, gave them the names of absentees, and proceeded with the roll call now containing the requisite number for an official mustering. The stand-ins were: Sheriff S. T. Porter, Professor W. F. Mc-

Carron, Dr. John B. Cross, Dr. W. W. Grant, George Kelley, John Jackson, M. L. Luther (who had been a drummer boy in the Confederate army), Dr. James Nankiville, Tom Evans, N. Lockmiller, John Tuell, John Peters, and Roger Sherman.

Soon old Springfield rifles and winter weight uniforms were issued to the new company. By summer, the unit was allowed to have their own light-weight summer uniforms made. A Mrs. Barr made the shirts and put brass buttons on them. The unit was called "The Brandon Guard," after the adjutant general of the state at that time, and had blue silk ribbons with gold lettering of this designation which were worn on civilian clothing. The Opera House was used as an armory, and troops drilled on the town square. Young girls came to watch the troops drill, and they all went to Algood's Bake and Ice Cream Parlor after the drills for refreshments.

In 1902 state militia (as the national guard was then called) from throughout Tennessee camped in Athens, creating great excitement. The camp was set up in North Athens along Woodward Avenue and was named "Camp Louise" after the wife of the governor at that time, James B. Frazier. Mrs. Frazier was the former Louise Douglas Keith of Athens.

According to Keith's account: "Each man drew two blankets, two blocks of straw, two wax candles, two men occupied a tent. For a bed you put your 'poncho' down then spread your straw, placed one blanket over the straw, and then used the other one to cover yourself. Then the tent had to be ditched around to keep water from running into it when it rained. If you sat down you had to sit on the straw covered bed, as no one but the officers had chairs in their tents." Keith then reported that it was the first night's sleep on the ground for most of the company, "but it did not make any sick."

Except for a misunderstanding about which guard station would let troops from the unit back into camp after a late trip to Algood's that ended with Keith and some of his friends in the guardhouse, the camp was uneventful. The governor and his wife came to town for a large reception. "Troop B," a crack cavalry unit from Chattanooga, arrived to add to the festivities, and according to Keith "the girls of town surely fell for the troops with their good looking uniforms, spurs and sabers." Beyond a doubt, times were much simpler then!

In early 1916 the Mexican revolutionary Pancho Villa executed 15 American citizens and raided Columbus, New Mexico. President Woodrow Wilson immediately ordered American soldiers under the command of Gen. John Pershing to capture Villa and put an end to the border conflicts. Serving as part of the Third Tennessee Infantry, McMinn Countians were on the Mexican border from July 1916 until March 1917. Their efforts constituted little more than a punitive counterattack, and although he was chased over a good deal of the Southwest, Villa avoided capture.

The time back home was short-lived, since by early August the local unit was recalled to active duty, spent a period of time training in Greenville, South Carolina, and sailed for France on May 11, 1918. The unit was engaged in combat on July 9 and became involved in the most decisive continual offensive of the war, which had them fighting almost every day through October 23, when they were finally relieved.

During this $3⅓$ month period, the army advanced from the low country of France and Belgium through the Argonne and nearly to the German border. The most significant moment came on September 29, 1918, when the formidable Hindenburg Line was smashed and the defeat of Germany assured.

In May 1918 another group of soldiers left McMinn County, ultimately destined to fight over much of the same terrain. This time, it was 90 men who represented the first "selective service" that the county provided. Training was done at Camp Pike, Arkansas, where the majority of the trainees were from Michigan and Wisconsin. They were fascinated by the East Tennesseans, and this fascination was heightened by John Derrick of Etowah who went through the camp giving speeches telling about how, when called from his home on Starr's Mountain to serve his country, he came riding out of the hills on a mountain lion and wearing a rattlesnake for a necktie. Several of the men, including Derrick, Charles Boone, and Vernie Smith, were from Etowah; Charles Gemblin, Oscar Kibble, Oscar Liner, and Luther Stephenson were from Calhoun, George Parkison was from Riceville, and John Kelley from Athens.

Their first combat was early October 1918 in the Argonne, and they soon pushed forward beyond the Meuse River in daily fighting. Liner, who was a barber by trade and often cut hair for soldiers while they sat on blasted tree stumps, and Boone were killed during this month and a half of battle. Like the McMinn Countians who came to this region 25 years later, they faced other obstacles in addition to the enemy—a flu epidemic killed nearly as many as bullets, shrapnel, and mustard gas.

On the morning of November 11 scouts were sent out to observe enemy positions as was customary. One group walked square into the face of a well-hidden German machine gun nest—they could have reached out and touched the barrel of the gun. Instead of firing, the Germans motioned for them to go back. At 11:00 A.M., word came that the Germans had surrendered—the men in the machine gun nest had already received the word. At noon, American and German soldiers met in the no-man's-land between their battle lines, shook hands, embraced, danced, and cried.

The unit was pulled back and that evening collected an enormous pile of wood to build a bonfire. With something of that fire still sparkling in his eyes, an 88-year-old veteran John Kelley, recalled how they sat in circles around the fire and sang battle songs to celebrate the victory. When the armistice was signed on November 17, the men marched to the Rhine River Valley where they served as occupation troops until April of 1919.

Perhaps the most decorated person from this area of the state was David W. Lillard, who had come from Decatur to practice law in Etowah in 1910. He was a leading figure in that community until 1941. Lillard commanded the Etowah guard company, took it to the Mexican border, and participated in 21 major battles in France before being wounded at Ponchaux on October 7, 1918. In spite of his wounds, he led his men to victory and received for his valor, among several other awards, the French Croix de Guerre and the American Distinguished Service Cross, bestowed by General Pershing himself. When Lillard returned to the county in 1920 a motorcade of several hundred cars escorted him from Athens back to Etowah.

Federal recognition of the local guard unit came on May 1, 1938, and by early 1939, as war clouds rose in Europe and the Pacific, the unit was fully enlisted. While numerous individuals fought in every theater and branch of the armed services in World War II, McMinn County became identified with the activities of the local guard unit, Company B, 117th Infantry, 30th (or "Old Hickory") Division. About half of the men were from the city of Athens and the remainder from the rural area. By the end of September 1940, the company had moved to Fort Jackson, South Carolina. The first officers were Capt. Herman L. Moses, 1st. Lt. Walter E. Moses, and 2nd Lt. Glenn Aytes. Soon Warren Giles and Zeb Sherrill were added to the rank of officers of the company. Company B had been at Fort Jackson only a short time before Staff Sgt. Charles P. Robinson established a reputation for operating the finest mess in the entire division. Col. Grant A. Schlieker assumed command of the 117th Infantry on August 12, 1942. Within a few weeks he moved Sergeant Robinson to regimental headquarters to operate the officers' mess. He did such a superior job that he had more influence with Colonel Schlieker than any other officer or man in the regiment.

Because the company was composed of men who had had military training, they were first used to train draftees. This continued until late 1943, when plans were made to move the company to England to begin preparations for the invasion of Europe. The company boarded troop ships in February 1944—an unforgetable introduction to ocean travel for most of the company. Many of them could hardly wait for sight of the first German who could be repaid for having made them endure this agonizing experience.

The company trained in England through late May amidst the friendliness of the English people and growing rumors and speculation about an invasion. At last, a tight lid of secrecy was thrown on the encamped unit the first week of June, and it became clear that actual combat was close at hand. Major Giles was the regimental intelligence officer and paricipated in the initial planning.

The first battalion of the "Old Hickory" Division landed on the Normandy Beach on "D Day + 6." They moved a short distance inland, dug in, and waited. Finally, on June 20, the enemy was engaged, and Pvt. Wayne E. Lavender became the first battle casualty.

The first three weeks of July found Company B (code name "Curlew Baker") engaged in what came to be their most difficult moment of the entire war: the hedgerows between the Vire River and the critical German stronghold at St. Lô. Crossing the Vire would be the first real battle, but until St. Lô could be captured there would be no significant "break-out" from the beachhead.

Beyond the fields and orchards inland from the Normandy beach the French countryside was crisscrossed by earthen dikes, tree-covered and sometimes ten feet high, that had been raised over the centuries of farming and construction of roads and drainage ditches. A War Department document from the period reported that in a typical eight-square-mile section of Normandy there were more than 3900 hedged enclosures. They were perfect for tanks, machine gunners, and riflemen to hide behind, and almost completely impregnable by conventional means of warfare. A successful day's fighting could easily be measured in feet and yards—and lives lost.

On July 7 the Vire River crossing took place and the initial battle to break out of the Normandy beachhead was under way. Company B played a large part in this crossing. Capt. Edward R. Friday, commander of the company, was wounded and Lt. Daniel L. Sullivan, Jr., assumed command. By nightfall, after the Germans had counterattacked but been repulsed, Company B and the remainder of the 117th Infantry had firmly established its bridgehead. On July 9 the Germans counterattacked once more, this time combining infantry with tanks from the Panzer Lehr Division; they were repulsed with heavy losses. On July 12 Lt. Sullivan was wounded and Lt. Robert C. Spiker from Morgantown, West Virginia, assumed command for the remainder of the war.

With the mixed blessing of a saturation air bombardment—often the pilots bombed and strafed their own infantry—the victory was finally won by July 19. The battle had been costly. Of the original 3240 riflemen in the division, perhaps as many as 75% were injured or killed.

The next major action took place at Mortain and St. Barthélemy, where a German counterattack of four panzer divisions and all kinds of artillery and infantry units were thrown into an attack that was designed to do nothing less than drive the Allies back to the sea. But "Old Hickory" stood in the breach, and while sustaining great losses—Company C was all but wiped out—held its ground. In postwar interviews, according to Lt. Col. J. B. Owen, Jr., of Calhoun, the leading German commanders Jodl, Keitel, and Kesselring considered the stand at Mortain as a turning point that led to the ultimate defeat of the Third Reich.

The Siegfried Line along the western frontier of Germany had been designed as an impenetrable last line of defense which would in all likelihood never have to be used. In case it was, it had been fortified with some of the best soldiers and most modern war technology available. By early October 1944 "Old Hickory" had arrived and begun its attack. Company B comprised the "valiant men" at the forefront of the battle who were assigned the painful task of destroying three concrete-encased enemy gun emplacements called "pill boxes." They captured their three and two more. October 2 was a bloody day for Company B, when it suffered 30 casualties. After six more days of fighting, Company B breached the Seigfried Line.

In December Company B reached the Forest of Ardennes and faced an obstacle as grievous as the hedgerows and the concrete pill boxes—winter. In fact, the winter of 1944–45 was one of the harshest on record. Men fell to frostbite almost as rapidly as they had to bullets. Veterans recall digging small foxholes, barely big enough for two men, spreading one poncho and overcoat on the ground, lying beside each other, and placing a second coat on top. Enough body heat was generated to provide warmth.

Into the midst of these desperate circumstances, Germany launched its most famous last ditch effort to turn the Allied tide, the Battle of the Bulge. Again, the 30th Division was at the center of the fighting. Veterans can recall being rushed in blacked-out truck convoys through the frigid night into areas that were thought to be secure. Massed armor moved all around them, and the infantrymen became nervous from being in a closed vehicle instead of in the open field where instincts of self-preservation which had been honed over the last months could be best employed. On more than one occasion on that night enemy flares lit the sky, and the men of Company B would tumble from the trucks and run for the cover of the tree line.

The radio voice of Nazi Germany, "Axis Sally," according to Owen, threatened "the fanatical Thirtieth Division, Rossevelt's SS troops, are enroute to the rescue; but this time it will be completely annihilated." The First SS Panzer Division, perhaps the best unit that Germany had left, zealously fought to make her prophecy come true, but again a German fighting force met its match and the battle was turned.

As Spring approached, the company received special training in river crossing for the next major offensive, the crossing of the Rhine. The Allied command expected intense resistance since this was the last natural obstacle before Berlin. The anticipated battle was so important that generals Dwight Eisenhower and William Simpson visited with the troops on the night of March 23, 1945. In Owen's record, when Sgt. Leroy Summers of Company B's second platoon was asked about the chances of a successful river crossing, he responded: "General, if Company B can't make it tonight, you can give up hope for the whole Ninth Army."

The crossing was made with relative ease, and suddenly German prisoners were being taken in droves. Company B still had a major problem, however; they were moving so quickly beyond anticipated objectives that they were coming under fire from their own air support. Daily advances of fifty miles or more became common—quite the reverse of the dreaded hedgerows.

Finally, at the end of April, Company B took the city of Magdeburg on the Elbe River. Fully capable of advancing to Berlin immediately, the company fell victim to the widely disputed decision requiring it to wait for the Russians to complete their westward march across Germany.

Soon the company returned to the United States. The men were greeted in New York harbor by the beatific symbol of liberty's torch, which somehow burned more intensely because of the past year of their lives. By V-J Day most of the veterans were back in the county, ready to carry on their fight for freedom in an unusual way.

Company B was part of one of the most highly decorated fighting units in the entire war, which received two Distinguished Unit Citations, the French Croix de Guerre with Silver Star for the Siegfried Line offensive, and the Belgian Fourragere for the Ardennes campaign, that government's highest unit decoration. More enlisted men became officers from this company than any other national guard company in the U.S. Army; three became generals—John Calhoun, Warren Giles, and Carl Lay.

Three other men received distinction in another way—Jim Barkley, John Elkins, and Charles Hughes were the only infantrymen in the company to fight through the thickest of all the battles from the Vire River to Madgeburg without serious injury or battle relief. Participants in an amazing record of bravery, they were there every step of the way. Their "medal of honor" was the silver-wreathed blue and silver combat infantryman's badge.

Wars are always instances of man's inability to live at his best. Nevertheless, the virtues of courage, devotion, and honor give rise to heroic actions by otherwise peaceful citizen-soldiers. The record of McMinn Countians in the great world wars, including 3500 who participated in World War II, reveals a striking patriotism that future generations need to recall, take pride in, and be inspired by.

The Battle of Athens

McMinn County has always been politically divergent, and many times that divergence has become belligerent and even violent. The confrontations between the old Whig and Democratic factions before the Civil War on the town square at Athens were preludes to other political differences that have surfaced across the years. In addition, there has almost always been a spirit of competition between the various cities and communities in the county—in the 1950s, it was not unusual for a McMinn-Etowah football game to become a pitched battle, punctuated on at least one occasion by gunfire.

Sometimes this political radicality could be based on what were conceived as the highest of moral and human intentions. The extremely active prohibition and temperance movements, that actually moved women with axes to invade taverns in neighboring Meigs County, are a good example of this. Prohibitionists became active soon after the Civil War and organized groups like The Sons of Temperance and The Women's Christian Temperance Union. Speakers toured the county in a manner similar to the pre-Civil War debates. In 1909 a majority of citizens voted to become "dry" and, the bootleggers notwithstanding, the county has remained so until today.

A notable example of radical political activity took place in 1920 and is a certain hallmark for the county. After years of intense political maneuvering, the women's suffrage movement finally succeeded in getting Congress to propose an amendment to the U.S. Constitution. It remained for 36 of the then 48 states to favor the amendment and it would become law. By August of 1920 Tennessee had become the key, 36th state. The state legislature deadlocked twice on a vote to table, and the opposition forces, feeling that the resolution itself would fail, called for a vote. Harry T. Burn from Niota (who had voted to table) cast what turned out to be the deciding vote in favor of the resolution. Burn voted for the resolution because he had promised his mother that he would help. One of the most important and long-awaited movements in American political history was complete.

However, no political activity in the county's history has ever come close to rivaling those events which took place on election day in Athens in 1946. Those events have come to be known as "The Battle of Athens," and they constitute the single most discussed event in the county's history. Many citizens still recall the events of the period, and often their involvement in them, as if

Harry T. Burn of Niota on the steps of the capitol in Nashville following ratification of the Nineteenth Amendment on August 18, 1920. Burn is standing to the rear of the photograph shaking hands with Anita Pollitzer of Charleston, SC, legislative secretary of the National Woman's Party.

they took place yesterday. Stories of large radios being placed before windows as shields, the sounds of bullets riccocheting against buildings, people sitting all night on their front porches with loaded guns, and the sight of brand new cars being burned in the streets are told and retold.

It all began with Edward Hull Crump. He came from the most difficult of backgrounds—his father died in the great yellow fever epidemic of 1878 when the younger Crump was three, and the dreams that his family had had of becoming landed gentry in rural Mississippi had been crushed by Reconstruction. Like so many who had found their way there before and after him, Crump made his way to Memphis. His rise to success there was phenomenal. He soon owned the business he had first come to work for, married into one of the finest families of the city, began to amass what would come to be a personal fortune, and—most significantly—became politically active in the notorious Fourth Ward of Memphis. He became mayor in 1910 and served until 1916. By the early 1930s, Crump had established the most powerful political machine in the state's history, a machine which influenced Tennessee politics for the better part of the next half century.

Historians in the future will probably give mixed reviews to Crump's career and his use of power. To many, particularly in Memphis itself, he was known as "Mister Crump," the man who rode herd on a sinful "den of iniquity." To others, especially those who were adversely effected by the outward extremities of the machine, he was "Boss Crump," symbolizing an iron-fisted, dictatorial rule that was not beyond corruption itself. Crump supported the TVA and opposed the KKK, but he also knew every pragmatic political tactic that was needed to control the polling place and to profit politically from doing so.

In what has come to be called the "vote grab of 1936," those who were sympathetic to Crump came to power in McMinn County. Paul Cantrell, who was involved with the powerful banking interests of Etowah and aligned with the equally powerful Burch Biggs in Polk County, was elected state senator and essentially became the county's boss. George Woods, also from the eastern part of the county, was elected to the state legislature and, with backing from Crump, ultimately became speaker of the house. Pat Mansfield, a transplanted Georgian, was elected sheriff.

To pass a final judgement on these men and their activities is difficult. In one sense, they participated in the types of political tactics that were commonplace at that time. Their activities were not unlike those used in many other places throughout the country. In another sense, the harsh activities that were carried out, especially by a large "gang" of deputy sheriffs, had to have at least the implicit approval, if not even encouragement and direction, of the high elected officials. There was cooperation with bootleggers and gambling rooms when there were adequate payoffs.

There was extensive "fee-grabbing" from unsuspecting tourists and travellers through the area. The sheriff was paid $5,000 a year, but received expense money based on the number of persons jailed—in the ten-year period ending in 1946 those expenses had amounted to an almost inconceivable $300,000.

Control of the ballot boxes, however, was the key, and this was done in two ways—possession of the apparatus that generated poll tax receipts, and the actual counting of the votes. It was not unheard of to have the poll tax receipts handed out in wholesale lots along with bootleg whiskey on election eve, and to confiscate at the merest whim, the receipts from political opponents. Names from graveyards throughout the county were often prominent among those who had voted. The deputies were the enforcers, bullies—some had served time in the penitentiary—who took advantage of the men being away at war to run roughshod over the population.

However, the soldiers heard about these happenings and chafed at the bit to get back home and do something about it. Theodore White's research featured Ralph Duggan, who had served in the Pacific in the Navy and who came to be a leading lawyer in the postwar period. According to White, Duggan "thought a lot more about McMinn County than he did about the Japs. If democracy was good enough to put on the Germans and the Japs, it was good enough for McMinn County, too!" White also adds that when two men on leave from the service were shot and killed by suspected machine forces, the out-of-power veterans and their supporters could no longer remain silent.

Five veterans and one civilian met secretly early in 1946 and decided to enter a GI slate against the Cantrell and Mansfield group. Following a tactic that Boss Crump had tried in Memphis, Mansfield was leaving office and Cantrell himself planned to take his place. The sheriff's office handled large sums of money. Crump had been advised by friends, according to William Miller's *Memphis During the Progressive Era*, "that he owed it to himself to run for some office with generous fees attached before leaving his political career," and Cantrell was following something of the same advice.

A mass meeting was called in May which required GI identification, at which a nonpartisan slate of candidates headed by Knox Henry, a decorated veteran of the North African campaign and a member of a highly respected Clearwater area family, for sheriff was established. Secret contributions from local businessmen enabled the returning soldiers to mount a strong campaign. The biggest obstacle to the GIs was the popular feeling that, in spite of how people voted, the machine would count the votes. The GIs established as the cornerstone of their campaign the slogan "Your Vote Will Be Counted As Cast!"

On election day the largest number of citizens who had voted in years in McMinn County turned out, as did over two hundred armed deputies imported by Mansfield for the occasion. Each polling place had "watchers" of both parties, and soon there was conflict. In Etowah, a GI watcher asked that a ballot box be opened and certified as empty; he was arrested and jailed. There were several incidents in Athens. Walter Ellis was charged with a "federal offense" and jailed. A black man, Tom Gillespie, was not allowed to vote over the GI watcher's objection. In fright, Gillespie ran and was shot in the back. Bob Harrell objected to an underage girl being allowed to vote; he was severely blackjacked and had to be hospitalized. Charles (Shy) Scott, Jr., and Ed Vestal were trapped by deputies while ballot boxes were confiscated in a city voting place on North Jackson Street. Scott's father and Jim Buttram faced drawn-gun conflict with Mansfield and one of his deputies while attempting to get the release of the young men. Through the diversion created by Neal Ensminger coming from the *DPA* to get a vote count, the men were able to break through a door to freedom. In a hail of gunfire the crowd which had gathered began to dive behind and under cars for protection; the men escaped unharmed, but the boxes were gone.

When the counting began, the GI slate was comfortably leading by a three-to-one margin. It really did not matter, unfortunately, because boxes from the voting place mentioned above and one other important location were taken to the jail, where the only GIs present were securely behind bars.

In marked frustration, and distressed over what was beginning to appear as a foregone conclusion, the GIs met at their campaign headquarters where Johnson's Home Furnishings now stands. Suddenly two deputies appeared, flaunting their guns and badges, and commanded the crowd to disperse. Otto, Oley, and "Bull" Kennedy were brothers who never knew what it meant to back down an inch, especially in the face of such an obnoxious assault. Otto recalls taking all the threats that he could stand and then saying all that was needed to be said—"Bull, let's get 'em!" In the ensuing riot, five deputies were disarmed, beaten, and eventually taken outside of town, stripped of their clothing, and sent on their way back to Georgia. These deputies, if in fact they did as they were told, were the lucky ones.

The problem of the ballot boxes still remained, and there was the additional problem that the GIs had now, in fact, breached the law. By morning, Cantrell could bring in reinforcements, perhaps even the national guard. If there was going to be a resolution of the situation, it had to take place immediately.

By early evening, quietly, the veterans had armed themselves with the best weapons available in the local national guard armory. Some rumors remain that they had surreptitiously purchased 100,000 rounds of ammunition for shotguns and slipped these into town. Knowing little about military tactics, the machine enforcers congregated in the county jail and made the critical mistakes of leaving the veterans a perfect, high-ground vantage point across the block. One shot from the jail, which in previous years would have been enough to disperse any objectionable crowd, was answered by a volley of fire that continued for hours. Years later, young people who had heard the story could still go by the old *DPA* office on North Jackson Street and see bullet holes in the the walls from the battle.

By 3:30 A.M., the men holding the jail had been dynamited into submission, and by early morning George Woods was calling Ralph Duggan to *ask* if he could come to Athens and certify the election of the GI slate. White reported that "when the GIs broke into the jail, they found some of the tally sheets marked by the machine had been scored fifteen to one for the Cantrell forces." When the final tally was completed, Knox Henry was elected sheriff, a good government league was formed, and a solid reform movement was under way.

The day after, an almost holiday mood prevailed. While there were random acts of revenge, the majority of the people who walked the streets, examined the bullet holes, saw the burned cars, and listened to the stories were caught up in a euphoria that had not been experienced in McMinn County in a long time. When one of the men trapped in the jail was asked what he did in the midst of the gunfire, he responded "I got behind the big stove in the kitchen—if it hadn't been hot, I would have got in it!"

Newspapers and magazines throughout the nation carried reports about the event. *Harper's Magazine* sent Theodore White to cover the story. On a late summer's evening in the early 1960s a carload of tourists from Wisconsin drove into the town square. Suddenly they were horrified to be caught up in the sound of repeated gunfire—a plague of birds which were soiling everything near the square were being dislodged. The tourist asked anxious questions about what was taking place, and a uniformed policeman jokingly responded that "The Battle of Athens" was being fought again. The tourist turned ashen, said that he knew all about Athens, and supposedly "burned rubber" from the Robert E. Lee Hotel to the First Baptist Church, disappearing in a cloud of dust out Ingleside Avenue. The "battle" was one of the biggest news stories of the postwar era.

There is no way to judge the impact that the events in McMinn County had on the rest of the state and even the nation as a whole. Inspired by these events, others rose to end corruption in their own communities. A figure of no less significance than Estes Kefauver emerged from the region to challenge Crump and win. Kefauver came to be one of the most important political figures in the nation in the 1950s.

Freedom is repeatedly taken for granted, until it has been fought and died for—then it becomes precious. When freedom becomes precious, the *status quo* seldom remains unchallenged, especially when justice has been compromised. For a compelling moment on August 1, 1946, in McMinn County, freedom was

A partial view of Bowaters Southern Paper Corporation, the county's largest employer

precious. In retrospect, historians may find it difficult to assign labels of "good guy" and "bad guy" in the "Battle of Athens." Labels that designate "ins" and "outs" may finally be more appropriate. Nonetheless, this was the epic moment in the county's history, and myth has long since replaced—or at least obscured—the events that actually took place.

A Look Toward the Future

After World War II McMinn County underwent rapid growth and development. The entrance of Bowaters onto the scene in the early 1950s set the pace for the next two decades. Olin Matheson and Rust Engineering soon moved into the Calhoun area, Beaunit came to Etowah, and Westinghouse established a major plant in Athens. All of this, coupled with the fact that almost every existing plant in the community experienced expansion and new construction, meant that the industrial base of the county was growing rapidly.

The vocational complexion of the county changed accordingly. The soldiers typically did not return to the farm but instead entered the plants, factories, and businesses. Many stayed in the county, but many others commuted to Chattanooga to work at Dupont, Combustion Engineering, and other plants. Others went to Knoxville and Oak Ridge to work for TVA and Union Carbide, while still others worked on TVA construction projects throughout the valley to build the new power plants that attracted even more industry to the region. The agricultural base of the economy rapidly changed, although fine farms continued to exit.

This economic expansion, accompanied by the "postwar baby boom," meant that new home construction skyrocketed. In Athens especially, whole new "subdivisions"—the word had not been used before—sprang up in the Ingleside and City Park areas and required that the city school system expand. Later, the neologism "shopping center" was added, and the topography of the communities changed even more. New highway construction to Etowah and Englewood, plus a Highway 11 Bypass from Niota to Riceville, greatly enhanced travel. The new interstate highway system ultimately paralled the old ETV&G rail route and opened the county to a revolution in trade and commerce much as the railroad had done a century before. Today the "Golden Arches," Holiday Inns, and almost every other symbol of major metropolitan centers are to be found right in the heart of the county.

In many respects, it seems that the community has become decentralized and somehow that it has lost the focal points that it may have had in earlier years. The owners of old family businesses could not always continue to hand their control down to another generation, as these succeeding generations may have moved away or somehow lacked the entrepreneurial zeal and creativity of the founders. Many of these businesses were bought by large conglomerates with corporate offices in distant cities. White Industries ultimately owned several local plants; the corporate giant, Pittsburgh Forges, bought Taylor Implement.

With the influx of industries from the North, new people came into the county and rose to positions of influence—economic, social, and political. There was a time only recently when it seemed possible to walk the streets of each town in the county and know almost everyone—that time has distinctly passed.

The greatest element of change may have simply been the growing American mobility. It became too easy to go to Knoxville or Chattanooga, Nashville or Atlanta. Their concentration of wide ranges of choice in purchasing, dining, and entertainment was simply more than the smaller communities could offer. Then, large corporate interests began to build shopping centers which further detracted from the central cities.

People seem to be searching for a new focal point around which to center the county. This may be too tall an order for an age in which television is rapidly completing the homogenization of society begun by Sears & Roebuck and Henry Ford. But as we conquer the ugly manifestations of provincialism—such as fear and distrust of anyone or anything different—we also lose much of the sense of continuity and tradition. The present age has made it as conceivable to view the county as an extension of Atlanta as it is to consider it an extension of Athens or any of the other communities.

It will take years for the new high schools to gain the same sense of tradition held by the old schools in the individual communities. No national chain of full-service department stores can rival the personal touch of Ed Self, Curtis Foster, and August Adams at The Men's Shop. It is almost impossible to conceive of the bright plastic, fast food places gaining the character of The Cherokee Huddle, Burkett Witt's—especially when it was in the old Cleage Building—or Riddle's when it was on the present Woolworth's corner with overhead fans replacing air-conditioning and milk shakes served in metal containers that held the better part of three full glasses. Undergraduates painfully watched the demolition of Ritter Hall at Tennessee Wesleyan so that a parking lot could be built, but the care given to Old College and Banfield Hall (now renamed Durham) has been more than worth the effort. Connections to the past can be preserved.

Attempts have been made to renovate downtown areas, and

The Etowah L&N Depot before 1910. This building has recently been renovated and is a local showplace.

in doing so to revitalize old business districts. Calhoun, the oldest town, has suffered the most dilapidation. The old main street looks beyond repair. Only one street remains with a hint of the gracefulness of old residences. Etowah, the newest, seems to have become progressively conscious of preserving the past. The renovated L&N station is beautifully done and a source of real civic pride. Perhaps its successful completion will become a catalyst for similar projects in other parts of the city.

Niota, perhaps more than any other community in the county, has retained a great deal of its original uniqueness and charm. The old business district, the main residential sections, and the railroad station are strong reminders of the past. Much of this resulted from the way that the original families and their kin have remained close to the community.

Athens has made a variety of efforts to reclaim the downtown area. Storefronts on both the north and south sides of the square have been redone and made quite attractive. The South Jackson,

The present county courthouse

Eastanallee area has been greatly renovated and a park constructed. Urban renewal has healed the scar of "Tin Can Holler," and new thoroughfares abound. The new courthouse, of course, is a striking centerpiece. An element is missing, however—the square's old character as a meeting place, a gathering place.

Ultimately, it is the people *together* that become the focal point of a locality. They lend it their character and style. Unfortunately, the forces of change that have swept the nation in the last two decades have made it difficult for groups of people to have the kind of community solidarity and identity that counties like McMinn once enjoyed.

New generations are coming on the scene. Generations are coming that may sense that something was missed in the postwar era's blind rush toward the twenty-first century. If they do, they will undoubtedly look for the kind of place that can be infused with their spirit. McMinn County continues to be exactly that kind of place.

Suggested Readings

Newspapers: The most extensive record of materials available on McMinn County is to be found in the archives of *The Daily Post-Athenian* and, to a somewhat lesser extent, *The Etowah Enterprise*. Both of these papers have published extensive, retrospective editions coinciding with the American Bicentennial and other important historical dates.

Public Libraries: The local history resources available at both the Athens and Etowah public libraries are limited. A few short personal memoirs are available. The McMinn County Historical Museum has been established on the campus of Tennessee Wesleyan College, and is becoming a center for an increasing historical consciousness in the county.

Resource Persons: James Burn at Edgewood Farm in Niota would be an excellent contact person for futher information, as would J. Neal Ensminger of *The Daily Post-Athenian*.

Books and Articles
Campbell, Mary. *The Attitude of Tennesseans toward the Union*. New York: Vantage Press, 1961.
Coulter, E. M. *William G. Brownlow: Fighting Parson of the Southern Highlands*. Knoxville: University of Tennessee Press, 1971.
Dykeman, Wilma: *Tennessee: A Bicentennial History*. New York: Norton, 1975.
Goodspeed, Weston A., et al. *History of Thirty East Tennessee Counties, with Biographical Sketches* (1887). rpt. Nashville: Charles and Randy Elder, 1972.
Hard Times Remembered: A Study of the Depression in McMinn County. ed. Bill Akins and Genevieve Wiggins. Athens: McMinn County Historical Society, 1983.
Historical and Pictorial Review, National Guard of the State of Tennessee. (available in annual editions with pertinent ones from McMinn County beginning in 1939).
Keith, Charles Fleming. Personal Memoir, n.d., in Edward Gauche Fisher Public Library, Athens, Tennessee.
Lewis, Thomas M. N., and Madeline Kneberg. *Tribes that Slumber*. Knoxville: University of Tennessee Press, 1955.

Lindsley, John. *The Military Annals of Tennessee: Confederate.* Spartanburg, SC: The Reprint Co., 1974.

Martin, Leroy. "A History of Tennessee Wesleyan College." 1957 (available from the college, TWC Library, and Fisher Library).

Patten, Cartter. *A Tennessee Chronicle.* Chattanooga: The Author, 1953.

Sharp, John McClure. *Recollections and Hearsays of Athens: Fifty Years and Beyond.* Athens: The Author, 1933.

Temple, Oliver P. *East Tennessee and the Civil War.* Freeport, NY: Books for Learning Press, 1971.

Tennessee State Library and Archives. "Inventory of McMinn County Records." Nashville: State Library and Archives, 1964–. Unpublished typescript.

Tennessee Valley Authority, Industry Division. *Agricultural-Industrial Survey* of McMinn County, Tennessee. Knoxville: TVA, 1934.

Turner, Martha. "The Cause of the Union in East Tennessee." *Tennessee Historical Quarterly, 40* (Winter 1981).

Valliere, Kenneth L. "Benjamin Correy, Tennessean Among the Cherokees: A Study of the Removal Policy of Andrew Jackson, part 1." *Tennessee Historical Quarterly, 41* (Summer of 1982).

White, T. H. "The Battle of Athens, Tennessee." *Harper's Magazine*, January 1947.

Index

Illustrations are indicated by an asterisk following the page number.

Adams, J. B. "Ace," 99
Arnwine, Bart, 79
Arterburn, Lowell F., 103
Athens, 7, 20, 26, 29, 31, 32, 38–39, 44, 117, 120, 121, 123–124; banks, 21; battle of, xi–xii, 112–119; fires, 70; in 1850, 20–21; in 1870, 56–59; in 1920s, 60–64; in 1930s, 65–67
Athens Hosiery Mill, 41, 54, 61–62
Athens Mining & Manufacturing Co., 51–55
Athens Press, 103
Athens Roller Mills, 41–42
Athens Training School, 95
Athletics, 98–100
Aytes, Glenn, 108

Baker, Rose, 78
Baptists, 83, 84, 85–86, 87, 88, 90
Barkley, Jim, 112
Blacks in county, 76–82. *See also* Slavery.
Blackburn, Gideon, 91
Blair, Samuel P., 68, 69
"Blue Front," 73*, 74, 89
Bowaters Southern Paper Corporation, 40, 120*
Boyd, Spencer, 31
Bradford, Mary, 9
Bradford, James C., 29
Bradford, James S., 31
Brient, Jacob, James & Mortimer, 49
Brown, Buck, 99–100
Brown, Dillard, 90
Browning Circle, 103–104
Brownlow, Parson William G., 27–28, 86
Bryan, Retta, 75
Bryan, M. L., 75
Buchanan, Brice, 79
Burn, T. Harry, 113, 114*
Burn, J. L., 69, 70
Buttram, Jim, 117

Calhoun, 7, 9, 20, 31, 40, 67, 91, 120, 123
Calhoun, John, 112
Cantrell, John, 11–13

Cantrell, Paul, 115, 116, 118
Cantrell family, 74–75
Cate, A. M., 36
Cherokee Removal, 16–19
Chesnutt, J. W., 49
Chesnutt, Nannie, 49
Church of Christ, 90
Civil War, 28–39; early emancipation position, 23–24; Greeneville Convention, 26; impact of war, 31–32; newspapers, 101; referendum votes, 25, 26. *See also* States' rights controversy.
Clegg (Cleage), Samuel, 11
Coffey, Asbury M., 10–11, 46
Collins, H. A., 68, 70
Confederate units, 29–30
Cook, J. L. (Jake), 80, 87–88
Cook High School, 95–96
Cooke, James B., 30
Cooke, William Henry, 13, 46
Crescent Hosiery Mill, 41, 69–70
Crutchfield, Thomas, 11
Cumberland Presbyterians, 82–83

Daily Post-Athenian, 101–102
Davis, George Barber, 91
Davis, O. L., 74
Deal, Bob "Mr. Dirty," 100
Derrick, John, 106
Dill's Company of Vaughn's Brigade, 37–38
Dodson, Jesse, 90
Dodson, Oliver M., 39
Dotson, Walt, 79
Duggan, Ralph, 116, 118

East Tennessee & Georgia RR, 46–47, 68; first officials, 46; schedule, 47
Early settlers in county, 7–14, 20
Education, 90–100; of Cherokees, 17
Elkins, John, 112
Ellis, Walter, 117
Englewood, 49–50, 87, 99. *See also* Tellico Junction.

Ensminger, J. Neal, 81, 101–103, 102*, 117
Etowah, 43, 48–49, 72–76, 117, 120, 123; attorneys, 75; Carnegie Library, 76; churches, 88–90; early businesses, 73–75; health care, 75–76
Etowah Enterprises, 101, 103

Federal units, 30–31
Fires, 70
Fisher, R. J. Jr., 61
Fisher, R. J. Sr., 52, 53*, 54, 61
Foree, Drs. J. O., Ed, & Carey, 66
Foreman, James, 18
Forest Hill Academy, 91, 92*, 95
Forest Hill School, 66
Forrest, Albartus, 30
Forrest, W. F. & family, 69, 70
Fountain Hill Academy, 92
Froneberger, W. R., 75

Garwood, Sid, 51
Gatewood, John P., 32
Gettys, Frank, 42
Gettys, James, 47, 80
Gettys, Uncle Nelse, 80
Gettys, Tobe, 67
Giles, Warren, 108–109, 112
Gillespie, Tom, 117
Goforth, Dr. N. B., 92
Gouldy, J. A., 29
Grand View Hotel, 54–55. *See also* "Red Elephant."
Gregory, J. W., 51
Grubb, Wayne, 100

Harrell, Bob, 117
Hart, John, 5–6
Henry, Knox, 118–119
Hiwassee Academy, 91
Hiwassee Rail Road, 11, 44–46
Hiwassee River, 1, 3
Hiwassee River Bridge, 35–37
Hughes, Charles, 112
Hughes, Joe, 34

Indians, 3–5, 16–19, 90–91
Industrial development, 40–75, 121
Ivins, Dan, 75
Ivins, Samuel P., 44, 101

Jackson, Amos, 80
Jackson, R.C., 44
Jarnigan, Hamilton, 42
Johnson, Charles, 87

Johnson, Harper, 80–81

Kefauver, Estes, 13, 119
Keith, Charles F. Jr., 63, 104
Keith, Charles Fleming, 13–14, 20
Keith, Elliot, 42–43
Keith, William, 79
Keith Memorial Church, 13, 86, 102
Kelley, John, 107
Kennedy brothers, 74, 118
King, Horace, 80
Knox, Glenn "Mutt," 98–99

Land, J. R., 87
Lane, Isaac & Tidence, 14, 84
Lane, James T., 27, 34
Lavender, Wayne E., 109
Lay, Carl, 112
Lee Highway, 64–65
Lewis, J. N., 73
Lillard, David W., 75, 107–108
List, Gussie Rose, 90
Lowry, William, 20
Lowry, Willie, 29

McClary, Dr. Spenser, 75–76
McDermott, W. P. H., 29
McGaughey, John, 26, 39
McKinney, Frank, 73, 103
McMinn, Joseph, 14–15
McMinn County: courthouses, 11, 12*, 124*; first officials, 20; map, 2; organization of, 20; 1834 population, 20
McMinn County High School, 96

Mansfield, Pat, 115, 117
Matlock, Isaac, 79
May, M. R., 26
Mayfield, Jessie, 11
Mayfield Dairy Farms, 60, 61*
Meigs, Return J., 15, 21, 91
Methodists, 83–84, 86–87, 88, 89, 91, 96–97
Miller, M. M., 51
Mills, early, 41–43
Moses, Herman L., 108
Moses, Walter E., 108
Mount Harmony Select School, 92–94
Mouse Creek (Niota), 21, 30, 47, 68, 70–71, 92; early merchants and settlers, 21
Mouse Creek Academy, 69, 92, 93*

Nankiville, Dr. J. R., 66, 104

McMinn

Nash, W. E., 77–78, 81–82
National Guard; 1901 volunteers, 104; police action in Mexico, 106
Neal, John R., 29
Neil, John C., 30
Newspapers, 100–103
Nichols, J. O., 75
Nineteenth Amendment, 113
Niota, 68–72, 92, 123; Bank of, 70. *See also* Mouse Creek.

"Old College," 34–35
Owen, J. B., 110

Parker, Dr. P. E., 75
Powers, Ozelle, 94
Presbyterians, 82, 85, 87, 90, 91, 94
Public schools, early, 94–95

Railroads, 43–51, 68, 72
Rains, John, 73
Reagan, James Hayes, 44–45*, 47
Red Elephant, the, 54–55, 56*
Religion, 82–90
Rice, Charles, 67
Riceville, 21, 31, 67–68
Riceville Academy, 92
Riddle's, 122
Ridenour, Prof. J. C., 66–67
Robb, James L., 97
Robinson, Charles P., 108
Rogers, John, 91
Ross, George W., 39
Rowley, Erastus, 97
Rucker, E. W., 29

Sanford, 21, 67
Saulpaw, G. L., 41
Scheeler, Reuben, 79
Schermerhorn, J. F., 18
Schultz, H. L., 68
Scott, Charles Jr., 117
Senter, DeWitt C., 28
Seventh TN Mounted Infantry Regiment, USA, 38–39
Sevier, Elizabeth, 7
Sharp, J. M., 65, 80
Sharp, Mrs. Ruth, 90
Shelton, James, 9–10
Sherman, Gen. William T., 32–33, 36–67
Slack, Ephraim, 41
Slavery, 22, 23, 77–78
Spanish explorers, 6–7
Spence, John Fletcher, 97
Spradling, Daisy Rice, 103
Spriggs, Pat, 79
Springston, Isaac, 18
Staley, C. B., 70
Stamey, Henry, 90
States' rights controversy, 24–27
Summers, Leroy, 111

Tellico Junction, 48, 49, *See also* Englewood.
Tellico Railroad Co., 49
Tennessee Coach Co., 51
Tennessee Wesleyan College, 54, 96–98, 122. *See also* "Old College."
Thompson, Riley, 42
Todd, Donald, 75
Trew, J. W., 43
Tucker, R. L., 74

Unionists, 25, 26, 38–39

Vandivere, S. H., 74
Van Dyke, T. Nixon, 21, 32, 46
Vestal, Ed, 117

Walker, John, 5, 8–9
Walker, John Jr., 16, 18, 20
Walker's Ferry, 9, 91
Wankan, Fred, 101–102
Ward, Nancy, 7
Wattenbarger family, 34
White Cliffs Springs Resort, 50*–51
Willson, H. M., 70
Willson, Hugh, 70
Willson, William, 60
Wilson, C. H., 79
Witt, Burkett, 79, 122
Woods, George, 115, 118
Woods Memorial Hospital, 75
World War I, 106–108
World War II, 108–112

About the Author

Steve Byrum was born in 1947 in Athens and spent the first eighteen years of his life in McMinn County. Since that time he has continued to live in proximity to the county and to retain many family ties there.

His mother's family (Bradford) were original settlers in the Calhoun area, have a part Cherokee lineage, and trace their English ancestry to William Bradford of the Plymouth Colony. His father's family had been tenant farmers who came into the area shortly after the turn of the century from the northeastern part of the state.

Dr. Byrum is a graduate of Tennessee Wesleyan College, with a master of divinity degree from Southern Seminary in Louisville, and master of arts and doctor of philosophy degrees in philosophy from the University of Tennessee, Knoxville. He is presently assistant dean of humanities and associate professor of philosophy at Chattanooga State Community College, and has written extensively in many areas.

He is married to the former Phyllis Hughes of Athens, whose ancestry is Henderson, Frye and Kelley. They have two children, Philip and Meredith, and live in Chattanooga.